SUSTAINABLE HOMES

LINKS

Autor: Pilar Chueca
Edición 2009

© Carles Broto i Comerma
Jonqueres, 10, 1-5
08003 Barcelona, España
Tel.: +34 93 301 21 99
Fax: +34-93-301 00 21
E-mail: info@linksbooks.net
www.linksbooks.net

SUSTAINABLE HOMES

LINKS

Index

In recent years the construction industry has become increasingly aware of the importance of reducing environmental impact. Since architecture is an art in which habitable spaces are created and a relationship between man and his environment is forged, it has logically become a discipline that, at times, embraces environmentally friendly strategies. However, many architects continue to ignore the problems, which affect the health of our planet, and continue to pollute in the name of architecture. Though construction in many cases can still largely be seen as a stain on the landscape, many ecologically aware architects are now taking a stand against this tendency and exploit the advantages offered by sustainable architecture. The use of ecological or recycled materials, self-sufficient energy systems and passive systems for temperature control without using energy-consuming heating systems can transform a building into something more than just an artificial volume in the landscape. Architecture is, at last, creating spaces where construction and nature respect one other.

This publication provides a sample of projects that, through their originality, boast highly sustainable designs. These designs harmoniously combine nature with design to provide beautiful spaces where the inhabitants can both live in and care for the environment.

This wide and varied selection includes projects by famous architects such as Rick Joy, Jennifer Siegal and Marmol Radziner, all of which show that ethics in architecture are essential, if we want to increase environmental awareness and create a sustainable world.

Loblolly House

Taylors Island, Maryland

Photographs:
Barry Halkin

Named for the tall pines that characterize its site on the Chesapeake Bay, this 1800 square-foot single family residence seeks to deeply fuse the natural elements of this barrier island to architectural form. Positioned between a dense grove of loblolly pines and a lush foreground of saltmeadow cordgrass and the bay, the architecture is formed about and within the elements of trees, tall grasses, the sea, the horizon, the sky and the western sun that define the place of the house.

The foundations are themselves trees, timber piles, at once pragmatic and poetic. Pragmatic because they minimize the disruption to the ground and poetic because the dwelling is literally founded on the tree - it is a house among and within the trees.

The idea of an elemental architecture extends to the method of assembly. The house is composed entirely of off-site fabricated elements and ready-made components, assembled from the platform up in less than six weeks. Specification is no longer conceived and structured about the sixteen divisions of the CSI that organizes thousands of parts that make up even a small house. Instead, the conception and detailing are formed about four new elements of architecture: the scaffold, the cartridge, the block and equipment. The aluminum scaffold system, coupled with an array of connectors, provide both the structural frame and the means to connect cartridges, blocks and equipment to that frame with only the aid of a wrench.

The assembly process begins with off-site fabricated floor and ceiling panels, termed "smart cartridges." They distribute radiant heating, hot and cold water, waste water, ventilation, and electricity through the house. Fully integrated bathroom and mechanical room modules are lifted into position. Exterior wall panels containing structure, insulation, windows, interior finishes and the exterior wood rain screen complete the cladding. The west wall is an adjustable glazed system with two layers: interior accordion-style folding glass doors and exterior polycarbonate-clad hangar doors that provide an adjustable awning as well as weather and storm protection.

This methodology confronts not only the question of how we assemble our architecture, but our obligation to assume responsibility for its disassembly. Just as the components may be assembled at the site swiftly with a wrench, so may they be disassembled swiftly, and most importantly, whole. Instead of the stream of decomposed debris that comprises much of what we are left with to recycle today, this house poses a far more extensive agenda of wholesale reclamation. It is a vision in which our architecture, even as it is disassembled at some unknown moment, can be relocated and reassembled in new ways from reclaimed parts.

Architects:
KieranTimberlake,
Stephen Kieran, James Timberlake,
David Riz, Marilia Rodrigues,
Johnathan Ferrari, Alex Gauza,
Jeff Goldstein, Shawn Protz,
George Ristow, Mark Rhoads
Fabrication & Assembly:
Bensonwood Homes
Construction Manager:
Arena Program Management
Structural Engineer:
CVM Structural Engineers
MEP Engineer:
Bruce Brooks & Associates
Civil Engineer:
Lane Engineering
Geotechnical Engineer:
John D. Hynes & Associates, Inc.
Interiors:
Marguerite Rodgers, Ltd.
Landscape:
Barbara Seymour Landscapes
Surface:
1800 sqft (168 sqm)

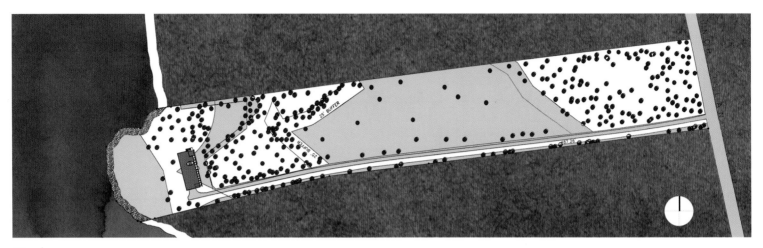

Site plan

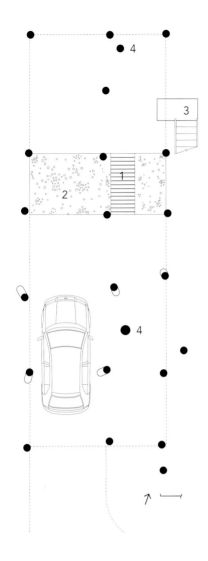

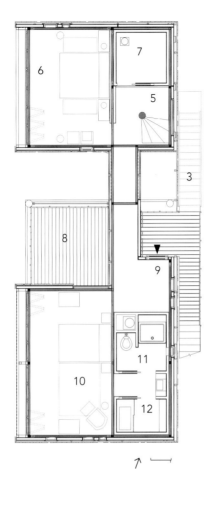

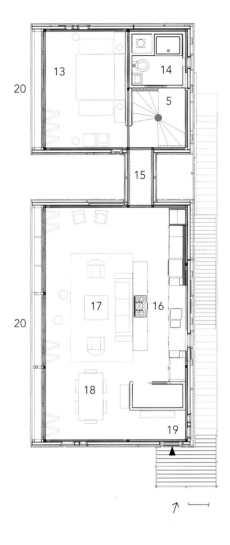

Ground floor plan

First floor plan

Second floor plan

1. Wood walkway
2. Bamboo and rock garden
3. Exterior stair
4. Mechanical piles
5. Spiral stair
6. Guest bedroom 1
7. Mechanical room

8. Outdoor deck
9. First floor entry
10. Master bedroom
11. Master bath
12. Closet / mechanical room
13. Guest bedroom 2
14. Guest bath

15. Bridge
16. Kitchen
17. Living room
18. Dining room
19. Second floor entry
20. High performance west wall

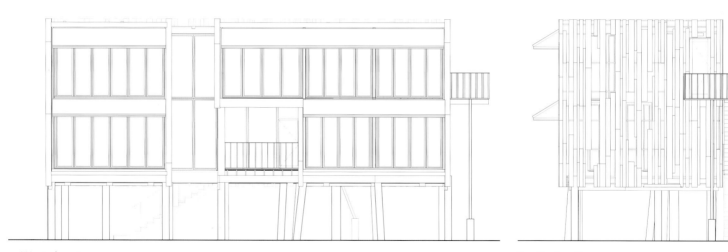

West elevation

South elevation

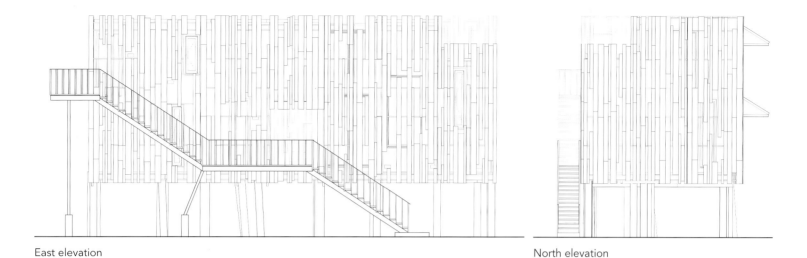

East elevation

North elevation

The foundations are themselves trees, timber piles, at once pragmatic and poetic. Pragmatic because they minimize the disruption to the ground and poetic because the dwelling is literally founded on the tree - it is a house among and within the trees. At the same time, the dwelling as seen from the east or land side is of the forest. The east wall is literally composed over a site photograph, with the abstraction of solid and void rendered in the staggered vertical board rain screen siding, sometimes positioned over solid wall and sometimes lapping over glazing to evoke the solids and voids of the forest wall. The land side elevation has no windows as holes in the wall nor any windows as the wall. Rather it has windows that are of the forest.

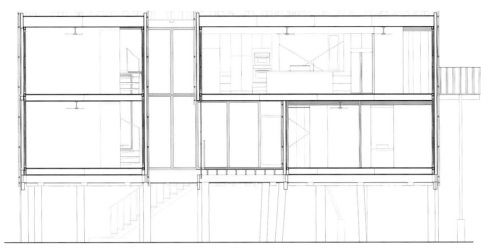
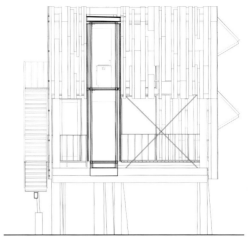

North–south section   East–west section

Malibu 5

Malibu, California

Photographs:
Benny Chan /Fotoworks

Vertically stacked and set into a hillside, Malibu 5 is a sustainable Modern home constructed of environmentally-friendly and recycled materials and designed to minimize energy use. The design was successful to the extent that the owners are contributing energy to the power grid during daylight hours.

Conceived as a passive solar house, it has photovoltaic panels and solar thermal panels for domestic hot water on the roof. The photovoltaic panels generate power for the house during the day. The amount of energy produced exceeds the owner's need and the remainder contributes to the local power grid. The house's power meter runs counterclockwise while the sun is up.

Ground-level concrete floors act as heat sinks, pulling in the sun's energy during the day and releasing it at night. They also provide radiant heating, making use of water heated on the roof.

Built as two, C-shaped rectangular bars – one two stories, one a single story over the garage – the house comprises four bedrooms and three bathrooms. The structures are separated by a courtyard that provides an opening for ocean breezes to cool the house. All rooms open on at least two sides to provide cross-ventilation.

The home faces the Pacific Ocean to take advantage of coastal breezes, energy-providing solar gain, natural light and views. Large solar-protected windows – the glass is double-paned, low-E and filled with hermetically sealed air – protect against the cold and heat. Shade is provided by overhangs from balconies. The large expanses of glass produce light-filled rooms and minimize the need for artificial lighting, which is controlled with motion sensor light switches.

The home's landscaping, populated mainly with drought-resistant foliage indigenous to California, mimics the surrounding sloped, rocky hillside. Rocks removed to prepare the site for construction have been recycled in walls, paths and xeriscape. Recycled water is used for drip irrigation to a limited degree.

The inexpensive scratched-plaster exterior is painted an earthy terra cotta color to provide a natural texture that smoothes the house's introduction to its environment. The color is inspired by the hue the architect found on a government building in the West African capital city of Accra.

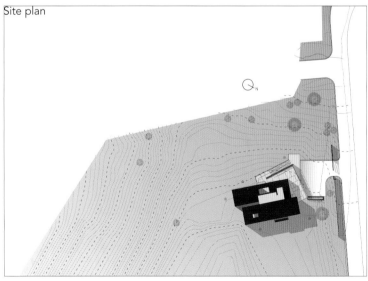

Site plan

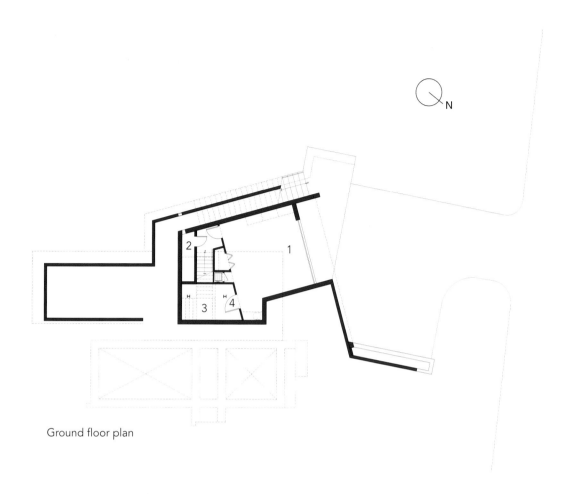

Ground floor plan

1. Garage
2. Wine cellar
3. Cellar
4. Mechanical room
5. Patio
6. Foyer
7. Living room
8. Dining room
9. Deck
10. Media room
11. Bath
12. Kitchen
13. Planter
14. Master bath
15. Study
16. Deck
17. Master bedroom
18. Walk-in closet
19. Bath
20. Bedroom

N

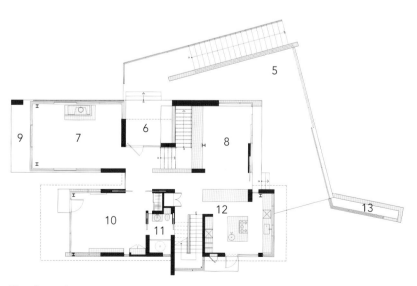

First floor plan

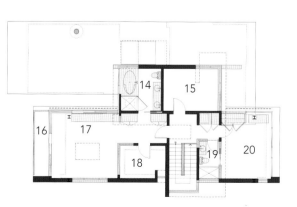

Second floor plan

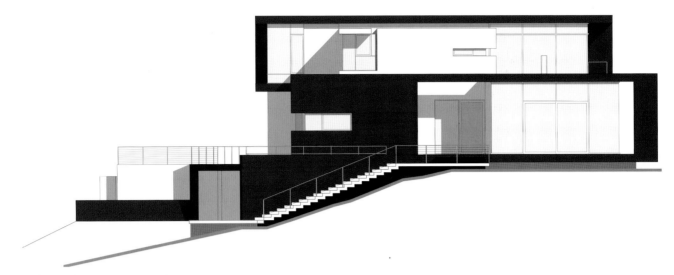

Northeast elevation

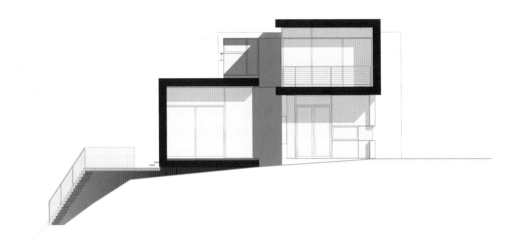

Northwest elevation

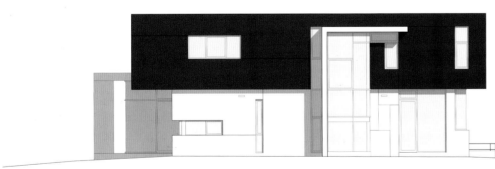

Southwest elevation

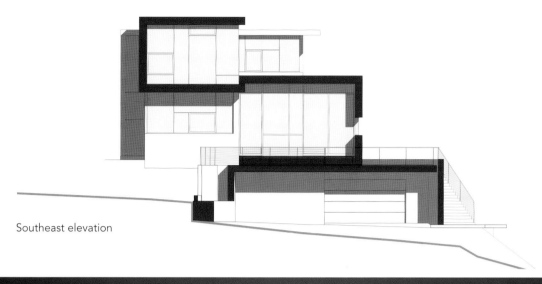

Southeast elevation

The inexpensive scratched-plaster exterior is painted an earthy terra cotta color to provide a natural texture that smoothes the house's introduction to its environment. The color is inspired by the hue the architect found on a government building in the West African capital city of Accra.

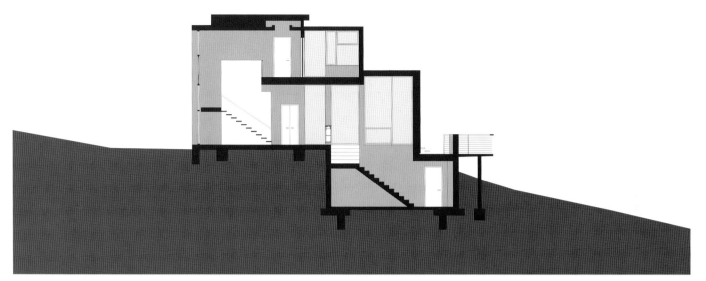

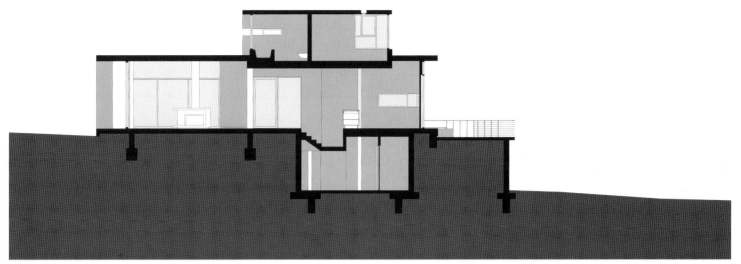

Large solar-protected windows – the glass is double-paned, low-E and filled with hermetically sealed air – protect against the cold and heat. Shade is provided by overhangs from balconies. The large expanses of glass produce light-filled rooms and minimize the need for artificial lighting, which is controlled with motion sensor light switches.

First LivingHome

Santa Monica, California

Photographs:
LivingHomes/CJ Berg
LivingHomes/Tom Bonner

Architect:
Ray Kappe
Production:
LivingHomes

LivingHomes is a leading developer of modern prefab homes designed by world-class architects. Their most recent model home, designed by the iconic southern Californian architect Ray Kappe, received a platinum rating from the U.S.GreenBuilding Council LEED for Homes rating system.

The two-story house was designed as a single-family residence with four bedrooms. It was constructed entirely from factory built modules, a form of construction that uses materials more constructively than conventional construction, and was erected on site over the course of just 13 hours. Environmental impact was considered at every turn, including the location, which is within easy walking distance of public transport and in a neighborhood where the use of bikes is very common.

The large doors, large glazed openings, and multiple exterior decks and terraces, which offer views of the surroundings, connect the project's inside to the site and allow the living space to expand to the outdoors. This flexibility between indoor and outdoor living spaces is traditional in southern California architecture.

The house has a very low energy profile in part because it has no forced-air heating or cooling. Instead, it features a radiant-floor heating system powered by a solar hot-water collector. The building also takes advantage of natural ventilation from the prevailing breezes, with an open plan and a whole-house fan that draws air up through the top of the home. The house was designed to optimize passive solar heating, with glazing designed to admit winter sun and balconies placed to shade the house from summer sun. Daylight from extensive skylights and floor-to-ceiling glazing provides most daytime lighting. On-site electricity is generated through the photovoltaic panels installed on the roof. These are connected to a system of batteries, which store any excess energy.

To recreate the open feeling of the space prior to construction, the project team incorporated a green roof into the project, which has been planted with native species. The site also includes a small vegetable and herb garden. Because the neighborhood was originally sited on sand dunes that were paved over for development, creating hills, the project site is sloped. Site drainage, stormwater use, and stormwater infiltration on site are important issues in this ecology. Rainwater collected from the roof, combined with stormwater diverted from site drains and swales, is stored in a cistern under the house and used to irrigate the gardens.

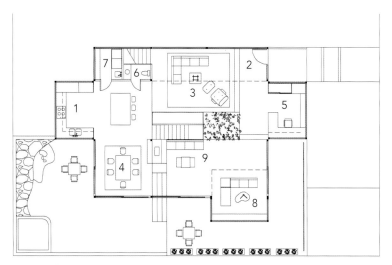

Ground floor plan

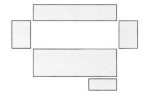

First floor plan

1. Kitchen
2. Entry/gallery
3. Living area
4. Dining
5. Study
6. Powder room
7. Laundry/pantry
8. Media room
9. Upper Living area
10. Master bedroom
11. Master bathroom
12. Guest room/loft
13. Guest bedroom

LivingHomes/Tom Bonner

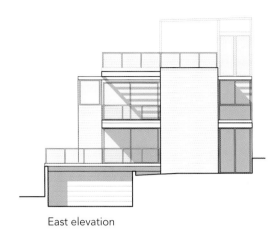

East elevation

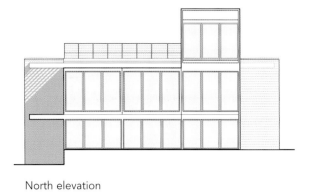

North elevation

West elevation

South elevation

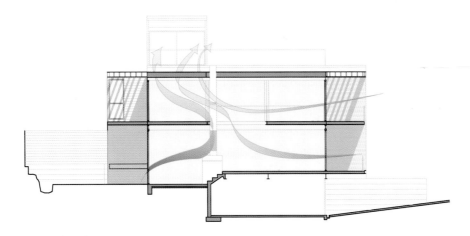

Section. Natural ventilation and solar shading diagram

35

The house was designed to accommodate the owner's current and future needs. The open plan allows for flexible use of space, and the bedrooms have sliding panels that allow the rooms to be connected to or shut off from common spaces, depending on the occupants' needs. This feature allows for fluctuations in family size, including children or elderly parents needing care. Because of its modular construction, the house could even be disassembled and moved to another location, should that become necessary.

Annie Residence

South Austin, Texas

Photographs:
Mike Osborne, Joseph Pettyjohn,
Ryan Michael

The house is located in South Austin, in Texas, on a small infill lot. It was built for two families and therefore is split into two living areas. The house consists of two pavilions connected by a glass hallway and sustainable principles of design have been incorporated throughout.

Each pavilion contains a central core made of steel stud frame covered with 8 x 20 cm (3 x 8 in) blue or red acrylic panels. These cores contain all the service areas of the house such as bathrooms, kitchens, utilities, and storage rooms to maximize efficiency. Concentrating most of the plumbing, heating & cooling and electrical systems avoids losing capacity through excessive turns. One pavilion contains two bedrooms and one bath while the other contains the rest of the program. Each volume is placed against the side setback of the property creating a central water garden in-between.

The reflecting pool becomes the focal point and all sides of the house open onto it. The walls against the sides of the property are closed, creating a courtyard layout. The two parts of the house are staggered to create a deck area in the front as well as a more private outdoor living area in the back, visually united by the translucent glass bridge.

The house is constructed from a modular steel frame. The frame is infilled with prefab thermasteel panels to minimize on-site construction waste. The structural frame is exposed, showing the construction process and articulating the house's façades. The repetitive modular method as well as the prefabrication allows for greater efficiency during construction. The 2nd floor in one of the pavilions is a viereendeel truss which acts like a bridge and minimizes the number of vertical structural supports in the 1st floor.

The flat roofs allow for terrace spaces, which create additional outdoor areas for plants and alfresco dining. The roof space is covered with a retractable awning made of shading tarp for nurseries and hardware from the nautical industry.

The house is influenced by different regions and cultures. Both the use of the roof as an outdoor living space and the shading devices are derived from Moorish architecture. The body of water and the spatial continuity between inside and outside were inspired by Asian architecture. The structural transparency of the volumes and the minimalist aspect of the interior were derived from Japanese pavilions.

Mike Osborne

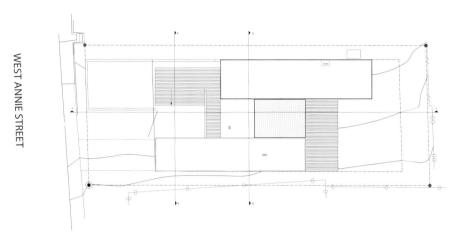

Siteplan

Joseph Pettyjohn

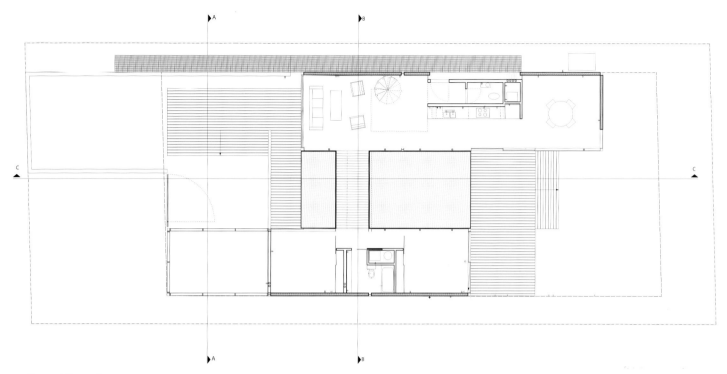

Ground floor plan

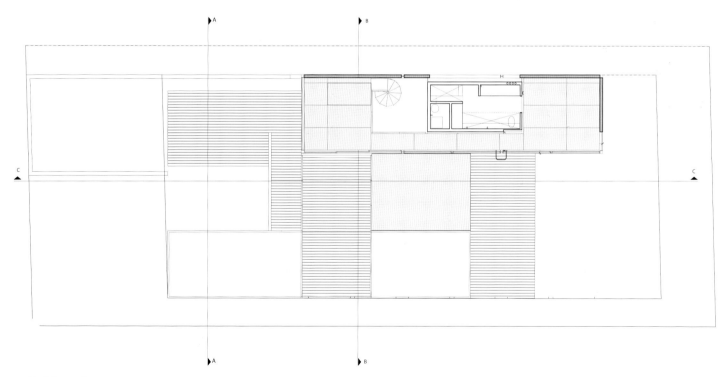

First floor plan

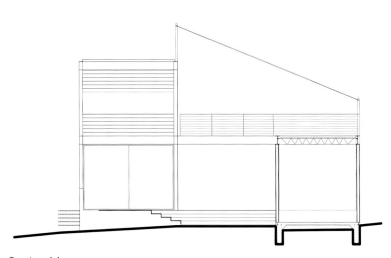

Section AA

Mike Osborne

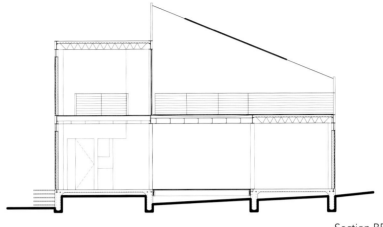

Section BB

Mike Osborne

Mike Osborne

Ryan Michael

Mike Osborne

Mike Osborne

Joseph Pettyjohn

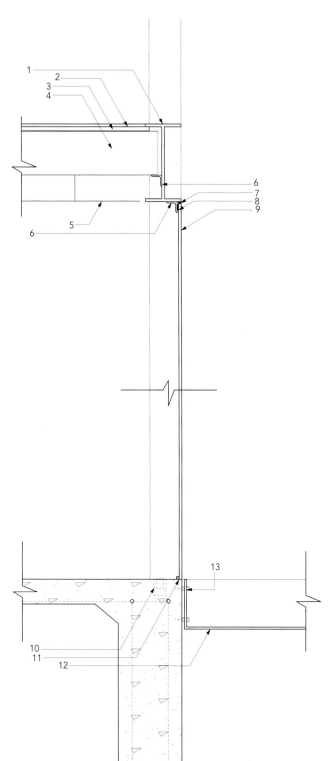

Ground floor wall section

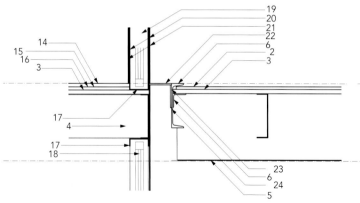

Acrylic wall - master bedroom

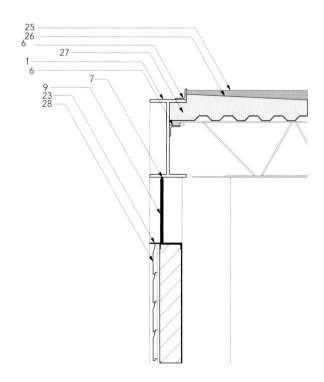

Roof - wall section

1. W-profile 14/38
2. Bamboo flooring
3. Plywood
4. Steel joist
5. Prefabricated steel panel
6. Steel angle
7. Dow corning 405 structural silicone
8. VHB tape
9. Tempered glass
10. Outlet box
11. Wood baton
12. Steel refl ecting pool
13. Bolt
14. Terra cota tiles
15. Thin set
16. Durock
17. Continuous steel runner
18. Fluorescent tube light
19. Steel stud
20. Black VHB tape
21. Acrylic panel
22. Glass
23. Steel plate
24. Fillet weld
25. Gravel
26. Base coat
27. Spray polyurethane foam
28. Cumeru siding

Mike Osborne

Mike Osborne

Mike Osborne

Residence on Beverly Skyline

Beverly Skyline, Austin, Texas

Photographs:
contributed by the architects

The philosophy behind this project was based on the notion that buildings are too often treated and designed as disposable goods, not built to last and only used for short periods of time after which they are torn down and replaced. The concept of progressive architectural firm, Bercy Chan, revolved around ideas of recycling a building, reusing natural and manmade resources and reclaiming the ancient ideal that buildings can and should be sacred places, especially the home.

The project began as a modest remodel, but turned into a full master planning for the site; including complete interior and exterior recycle, an addition to an existing 1970's home, as well as the reorganization of the garden.

One goal was to integrate the architecture with the native garden and creek at the bottom of the property. To fully enjoy the reclaimed views, the house is wrapped by exterior decks with glass railings. The architects found inspiration in the Kiyomizu temple in Kyoto, Japan, which sits above the landscape and provides panoramic views of the city.

In the spirit of reclaiming value, recycled materials are employed at every possible opportunity. The front façade of the house is comprised of recycled glass blocks, which were provided by the owner as a condition of the commission. The originally monolithic nature of the house is further dematerialized through the use of slats installed as rain screens. This wall assembly seems to dissolve the façade of the house, particularly at corner conditions.

The project also makes extensive use of harvested rainwater stored in pools and reservoirs to reconnect the house with its site. The water system lends a sense of drama to the intervention. A series of cascading ponds serve as part of the rain water collection system on a utilitarian level. On an aesthetic level they provide a peaceful transition between the landscape and the architecture. The ponds are made with salvaged steel sheets and poured in place concrete.

Architectural elements are treated as installation art work and sculptures in this project. For instance the front door is a copper box taking on characteristics from the Donald Judd sculptures. Gutter drains are made with clear Plexiglas tubing so the downward journey of water is appreciated and the rainwater re-harvesting process is better understood, the simple movement of water becomes an animating agent for the architecture and the landscape.

The selection of plants in the garden consists primarily of plants native to the central Texas region. This minimizes the usage of water, and follows principles of xeriscaping, i.e. landscaping that does not require supplemental irrigation. The garden is planned around existing mature trees and shrubs with various ground covers and perennials. The intention was to preserve the characteristic of the site as much as possible and retain the essence of a landscape native to the Edwards plateau in the hill country.

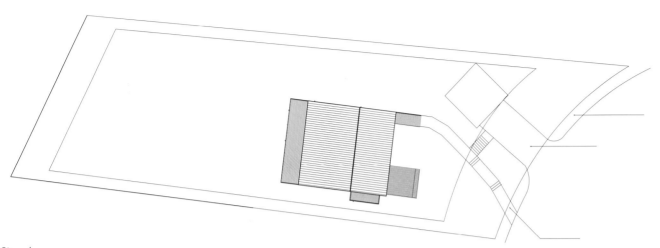

Site plan

1. Workshop
2. Storage
3. Bedroom
4. Game room
5. Bath
6. Master bedroom
7. Opening to lower floor

Ground floor plan

Second floor plan

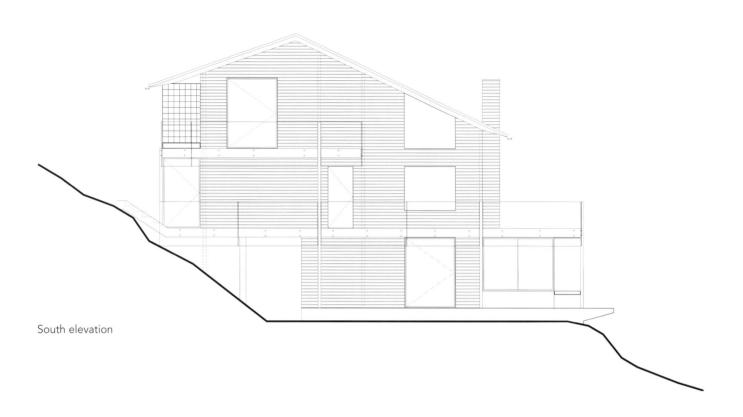

South elevation

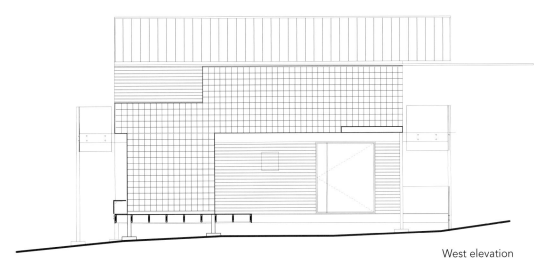

West elevation

As the original house was poorly sited, a large motivation of the design was to reconnect the house with its site by utilizing the steep topography to capture the expansive views.

Architectural elements are treated as installation art work and sculptures in this project. For instance the front door is a copper box taking on characteristics from the Donald Judd sculptures. Gutter drains are made with clear Plexiglas tubing so the downward journey of water is appreciated and the rainwater re-harvesting process is better understood, the simple movement of water becomes an animating agent for the architecture and the landscape.

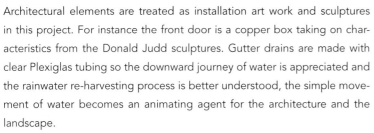

Glass block wall detail

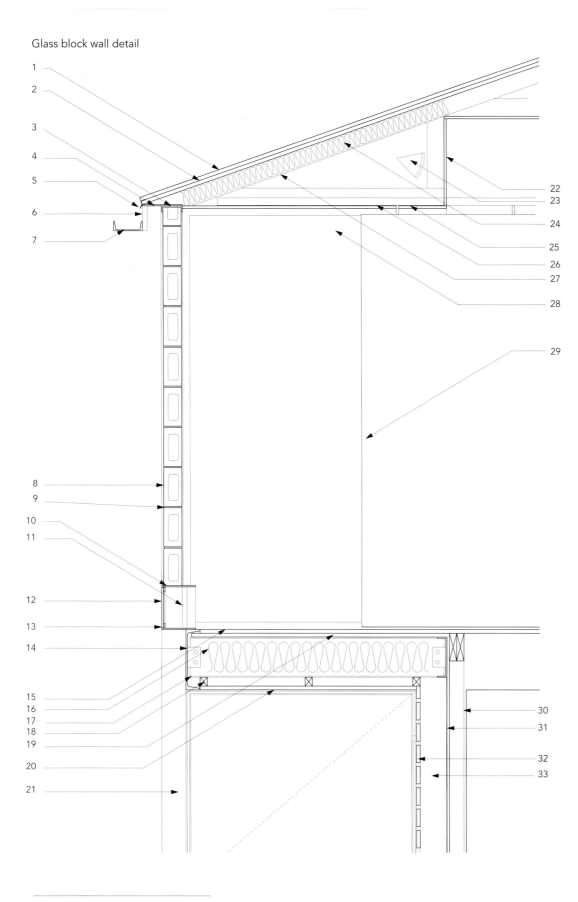

1. Screw down galvalum metal roof
2. Wood decking
3. Gage hollow metal channel
4. Steel plate soffit
5. Metal flashing
6. Steel plate bracing
7. Steel gutter
8. Glass blocks
9. Mortar
10. Mortar bed on steel plate
11. Steel tube
12. Tempered glass
13. Steel plate frame
14. Steel C-profile
15. Wood flooring
16. R30 batt insulation
17. Steel joist
18. Wooden blocking to recieve
    hardiplank soffit
19. CDX plywood subfloor
20. Hardiplank painted white
21. Steel angle
22. Translucent panel
23. Lighting
24. R30 batt insulation
25. Gypsum board painted white
26. Sliding door track
27. Rafter extension
28. Glass door beyond
29. Sliding panel to close bedoroom
30. Existing wall
31. Tamco peel and stick water barrier
32. IPE siding
33. Furring strip

Carter Burton

The Shenandoah Retreat

Warren County, Virginia

Photographs:

Daniel Afzal

The Shenandoah Retreat sits on a steep ledge with panoramic views of the Blue Ridge Mountains. The house was built for a couple who wanted a place to escape the city at the weekends where they could also invite family and friends. The brief was for a clean modern aesthetic that suits the site and takes advantage of the dramatic views.

The mass of the house is designed as a composition of smaller forms that follow the site contours. The scale of the house grows from an open deck area at the west side of the clearing, to a four-story tower scaled to relate to that of the east tree line. Beyond the tower, the one-story master bedroom wing nestles into the woods for a more intimate setting. In general, all main rooms face south, and have angled glass walls for optimal solar exposure and solid north walls to provide a thermal barrier against winter wind.

On entering the house the stair tower emerges as the central organizing element, separating the private master bedroom wing from the open kitchen, living, and dining areas of the Great Room. Intended as a vertical gallery for the couple's art collection, the tower and its integrated fireplaces create a central hearth element. In the Great Room high clerestory windows bring in north light. Along the walls, giant custom sliding panels are used to display the paintings. The opposite wall features a steel frame and glass wall tilted towards the south, leaving a place for the informal dining area.

The lower level has a large family room, mud room, and guest suite with glass doors that open onto a large terrace, thus creating a strong connection to the outside. By locating the second bedroom beneath the deck, more living space is gained without increasing the scale of the house. The combination wood and concrete deck connects the kitchen area to the screened Porch pavilion. Outdoor cooking and entertaining revolve around a built-in concrete grill center. Roof run-off is collected in an adjacent river-rock drain bed and concrete basin.

Exposed interior concrete walls provide structure and support for a concrete floor. Stress-skin walls, a steel structural frame, and aluminum windows comprise the house's structure, while vertical exterior cedar siding adds warmth and texture. All of the windows and structural materials were manufactured or fabricated within 30 miles of the site.

The structure benefits from many passive systems for heating, cooling and daylighting thereby reducing energy consumption, and includes an energy-efficient geothermal heat pump, and radiant floor heating. In the winter months, the living room is warmed by the low sun through the south facing windows. Exposed concrete floors throughout the home absorb and slowly release this heat. In the summer, large overhangs shade the interior of the house, and windows in the tower can open up to expel heat. When it is simply too hot to be upstairs or even inside, this seasonally designed house has a bermed basement and guest room to serve as a cave-like retreat from the heat.

The master bedroom wing and the entry hall have been built on piers to allow ground water to flow under the house.

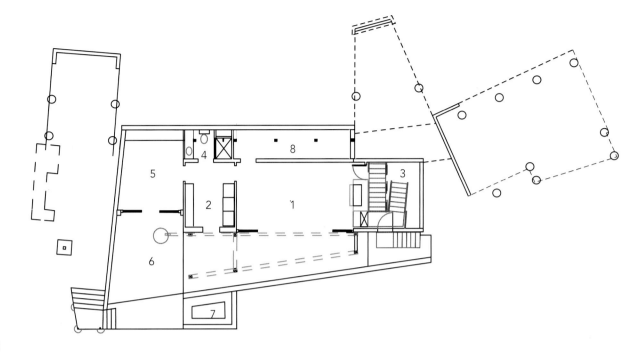

1. Living area
2. Laundry
3. Stair tower
4. Bathroom
5. Bedroom
6. River rock drainbed
7. Spa
8. Mechanical room

Lower level plan

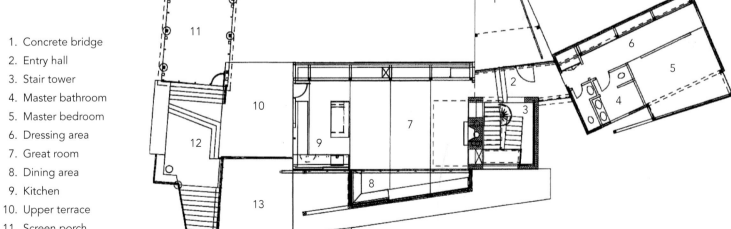

1. Concrete bridge
2. Entry hall
3. Stair tower
4. Master bathroom
5. Master bedroom
6. Dressing area
7. Great room
8. Dining area
9. Kitchen
10. Upper terrace
11. Screen porch
12. Upper deck
13. River rock drainbed
14. Spa
15. Lower terrace

Main level plan

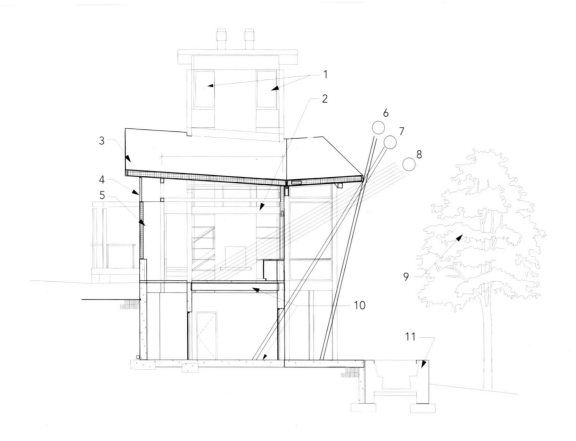

1. Chimney effect vent windows
2. Cantilevered concrete arms as extra heat sink surface
3. Cantilever sips, both sides
4. High north daylight
5. North privacy buffer storage cabinets
6. June 21st
7. Late march - mid sept
8. Dec 21st
9. Eastern trees block summer sun, allow for southern view to river
10. Radiant heat supplements passive solar heat sink concrete floors
11. Cyclyical latent cooling (no chemicals) in spa for 10 people. Sips cover w/Truck bedliner coating
12. Sips roof
13. Cross ventilation
14. Stepping lightly on sonotube foundations allows groundwater to pass through to nature below

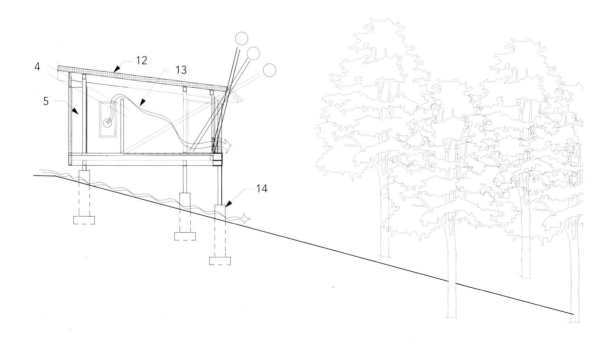

A custom terrazzo ground concrete jacuzzi is located on the lower terrace where the clients and their guests can relax and soak up these beautiful surroundings.

Exposed interior concrete walls provide structure and support for a concrete floor. Stress-skin walls, a steel structural frame, and aluminum windows comprise the house's structure, while vertical exterior cedar siding adds warmth and texture. All of the windows and structural materials were manufactured or fabricated within 30 miles of the site.

The lower level has a large family room, mud room, and guest suite with glass doors that open onto a large terrace, thus creating a strong connection to the outside. By locating the second bedroom beneath the deck, more living space is gained without increasing the scale of the house.

Farley Studio

Cleburne, Texas

Photographs:
Viviane Vives and MJ Neal,
courtesy of MJ Neal Architects, LLC

Renderings:
Jett Butler of Foda Studio,
courtesy of MJ Neal Architects, LLC
Structural insulated panels:
Steel SIP Fabricators
Tile:
Daltile
Surface:
228 sqm (2460 sqft)
Cost:
$ 150 000

The brief for this space was to create a painting studio and a residence for a couple who were not planning on having any children. One of the premises from which this project developed was the strict budget that the architect had to adhere to, which is why he decided to simplify where possible. Only the essentials were included in the program: a living room, kitchen, powder room and the studio were located on the ground floor, while upstairs accommodates the bedroom and bathroom.

The building's structure is a basic metal and glass box sat on a concrete slab, which at night appears to float above the landscape. Attached to the prefabricated steel structure are steel structural insulated panels (SIPS), covered with corrugated galvanized metal sheets, which provide enclosure and protection against the elements. Translucent polycarbonate panels have been fixed to the east and north side walls. They change appearance at different times of the day; on occasions opaque, at other times transparent. One of these panels opens the studio to the exterior allowing the clients to work on a large-scale. The panels can either be lit from the front or the back depending on the amount of daylight outside or artificial light inside.

The "Chinese box" stands like an object within the space in the middle of the building, separating the studio from the living room. The box houses the kitchen, powder room, and stairs on the first floor, and the master bedroom upstairs. A Chinese box is a container, which is used for valuables and contains sliding panels and secret compartments. In this case the sliding panels reveal or conceal the kitchen and the bedroom. Other openings can be operated when needed to open or close spaces. The box is also used to control the temperature in the space. When opened it allows the air to circulate and when closed warm air remains inside. This is the only space in the project where air-conditioning has been installed, a strategy that implies a significant reduction in energy consumption.

On the second floor, bar grating defines another slot for circulation and storage. Like the polycarbonate panels, the grating also changes in opacity depending upon the angle of vision. As a storage space it is particularly useful since its contents can be seen from the side, above, and below. The west wall is glazed from top to bottom in blue-tinted solar glass. The same glass is used on the south side and is shielded by the corrugated, galvanized steel skin. Long, low windows on the south side reveal views of knees, ankles, and nearby vegetation. A secondary steel structure defines the west patio and fire pit area.

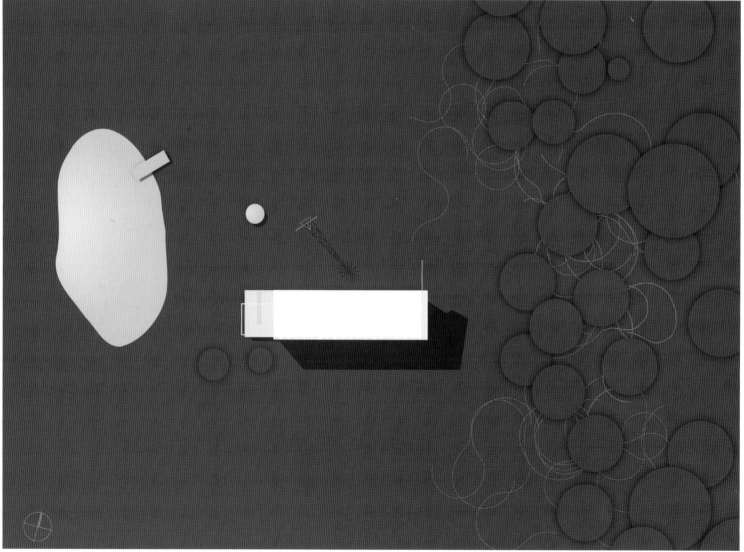

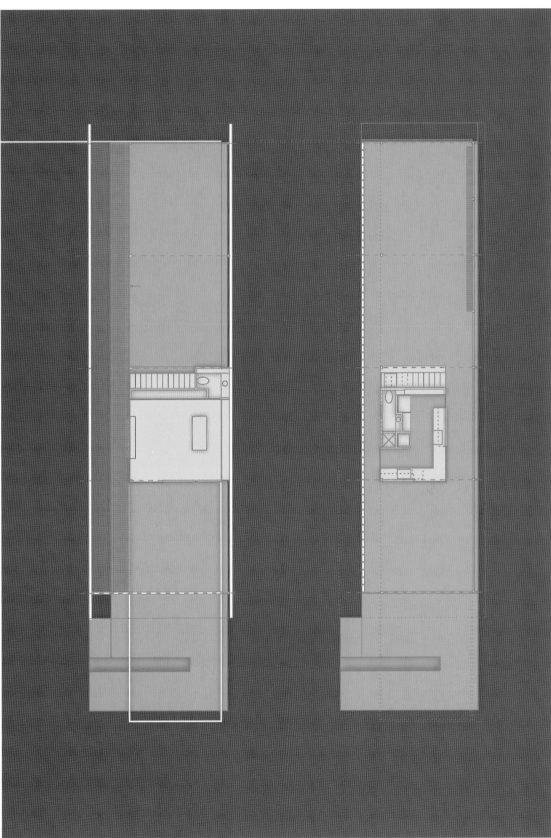

Translucent polycarbonate panels have been fixed to the east and north side walls. They change appearance at different times of the day; on occasions opaque, at other times transparent. One of these panels opens the studio to the exterior allowing the clients to work on a large-scale.

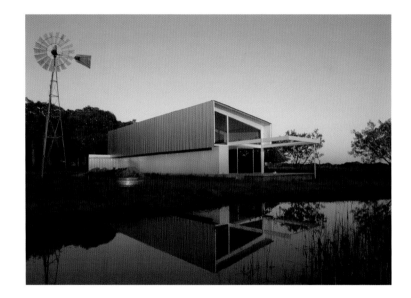

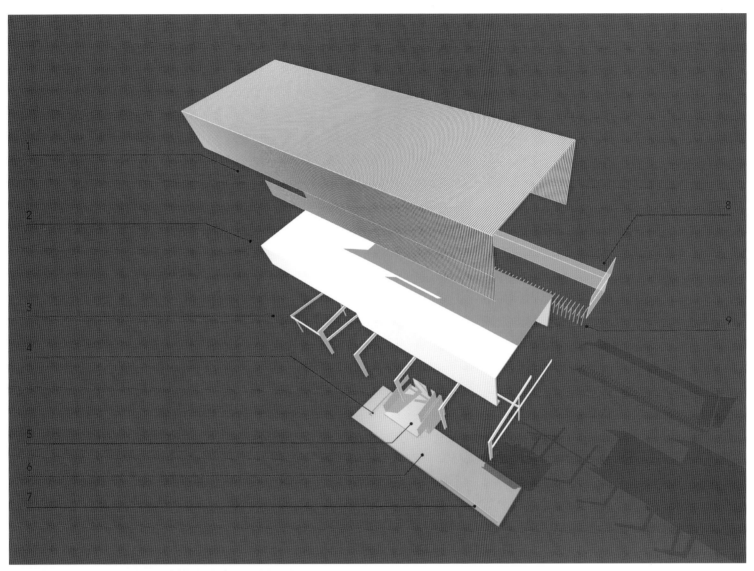

1. Galvanized corrugated metal
2. [SIPS] metal structural insulated panels
3. Pre-fabricated steel superstructure
4. Fire pit
5. "Chinese box", only mechanically air-conditioned space. Bedroom, kitchen, baths with sliding pivoting openings operated as desired
6. Concrete slab
7. Slot. Recycling of sand and other granulated material for artist works
8. Polycarbonate wall and soffit
9. Wood framing

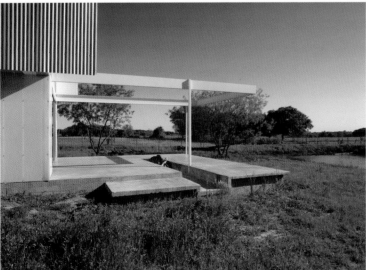

The "Chinese box" stands like an object within the space in the middle of the building, separating the studio from the living room. The box houses the kitchen, powder room, and stairs on the first floor, and the master bedroom upstairs. A Chinese box is a container, which is used for valuables and contains sliding panels and secret compartments. In this case the sliding panels reveal or conceal the kitchen and the bedroom. Other openings can be operated when needed to open or close spaces.

Solar Umbrella

Venice, California

Photographs:
Marvin Rand

Architects:
Angela Brooks and Lawrence Scarpa
of Pugh + Scarpa
Project Design Team:
Angela Brooks, Anne Burke, Vanessa
Hardy, Ching Luk, Gwynne Pugh,
Lawrence Scarpa
Structural Engineering:
Gwynne Pugh, Pugh + Scarpa
General Contractor:
Above Board Construction
Client/Owner:
Angela Brooks and Lawrence Scarpa

The Solar Umbrella Residence is located in a residential neighborhood of Venice, California, and sets a precedent for the next generation of Californian modernist architecture. This project saw the transformation of the architects' existing 60 sqm (650 sqft) bungalow into a 180 sqm (1900 sqft) residence equipped for responsible living in the twenty-first century. The architects carefully considered the entire site, taking advantage of as many opportunities for sustainable living as possible. Passive and active solar design strategies render the residence 100% energy neutral.

The addition shifts the residence 180 degrees from its original orientation. What was formerly the front and main entry at the north becomes the back. This optimizes exposure to energy rich southern sunlight. The solar panels that wrap around the south elevation and roof become the defining formal expression of the residence. Conceived as a solar canopy, these panels protect the building from thermal heat gain by screening large portions of the structure from direct exposure to the intense sun. Rather than deflecting sunlight, the solar skin absorbs and transforms it into usable energy, providing the residence with 100% of its electricity.

By removing only one wall at the south, the architects maintain the primary layout of the existing residence. A sizable addition to the south includes a new entry, living area, master suite accommodations, and utility room for laundry and storage. The kitchen, which once formed the back edge of the residence, opens into a large living area, which in turn, opens out to a spacious front yard. An operable wall of glass in the living area delicately defines the edge between interior and exterior.

Taking cues from the California modernist tradition, the architects conceived of exterior spaces as outdoor rooms. By creating strong visual and physical links between outside and inside, these outdoor rooms interlock with interior spaces, blurring the boundary and creating a more dynamic relationship between the two. The entry sequence along the western edge of the property demonstrates this concept. A cast in place concrete pool provides a strong landscape element and defines the path to the front entry. Upon reaching the entry, the pool cascades into a lower tier of water that penetrates and interlocks with the geometry and form of the residence. Stepping stones immersed in the water create an entrance path to the residence as the visitor is invited to walk across water. The distinction between outside and inside is once again blurred.

An unbroken visual corridor is established from one end of the property to the other. This transparency affords visibility from front to back and gives the structure an apparent lightness. Light penetrates the interior of the residence at several locations. A series of stepped roofs, glazed walls, and clerestory windows allow light to enter from different directions. The resulting play of light enlivens the more permanent and fixed elements of the design.

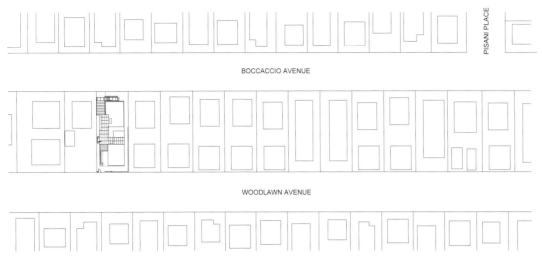

PISANI PLACE

BOCCACCIO AVENUE

WOODLAWN AVENUE

Site plan

First floor plan

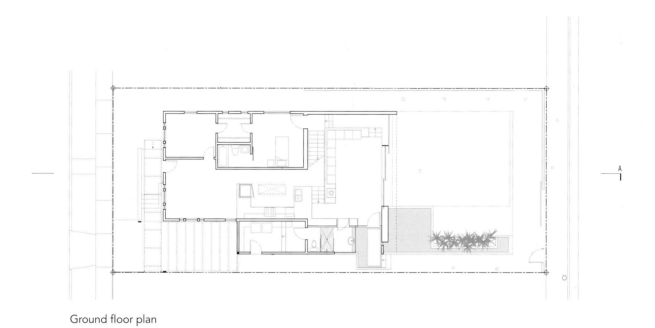

Ground floor plan

1. Living
2. Dining
3. Kitchen
4. Bedroom
5. Study

6. Bathroom
7. Closet
8. Waterpond
9. Bamboo planter
10. Bath

11. Laundry
12. A.V. center
13. Master bedroom
14. Master bathroom
15. Shower/tub

16. Closet
17. Patio
18. Roof
19. Skylight

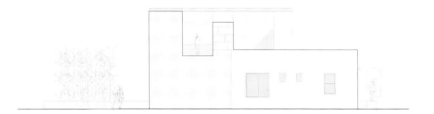

North elevation

West elevation

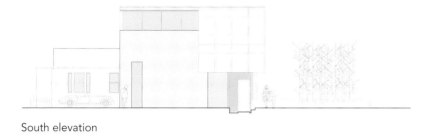

South elevation

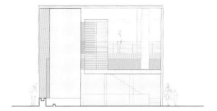

East elevation

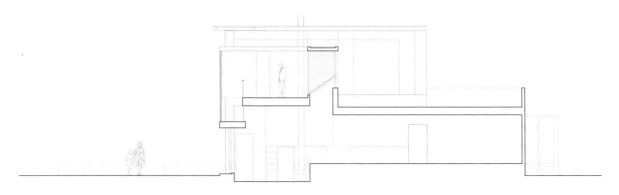

Section A

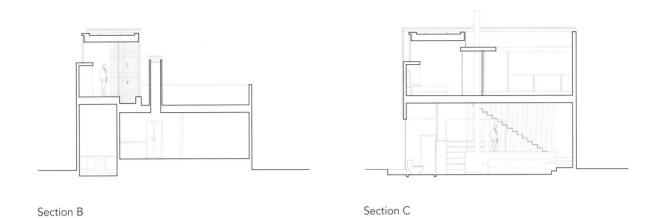

Section B   Section C

The master suite on the second level reiterates the strategy of interlocking space by opening onto a deep covered patio, which overlooks the garden.

Dome House

Ojai, California

Photographs:
Gregory Goode

The aim with this home was to create a structure that would have little impact on the environment, would be relatively inexpensive and could be easily disassembled, transported and reassembled in a different location. The couple, Shawn Hausman and his partner, Jessica Kimberly, who were to live in the house with their eleven-year-old son, wanted to explore alternative options to traditional housing typologies. The result is this prefabricated geodesic dome, which meets all their requirements.

The design of the geodesic dome structure is the brainchild of the late Buckminster Fuller, considered to be a visionary and pioneer in the field of affordable housing and prefabricated construction. He inspired the creation of the Buckminster Fuller Institute (http://www.bfi.org), a foundation set up at the time of his death to encourage and implement innovative designs that allow for sustainable living. Geodesic domes are able to cover more space without internal supports than any other kind of enclosure, and become proportionally lighter and stronger as they grow in size. The company, Pacific Domes, designs and produces geodesic domes and provided the kit for this home.

The dome measures 13 m (44 ft) across and at its highest point rises to 6.5 m (22 ft). It rests on wooden decking supported by concrete footings, which offers excellent views of the surrounding landscape – the ocean and the mountains – and is the perfect spot for relaxing outside and soaking up this spectacular environment. An event tent erected on the deck, in keeping with the style of the house, provides shade from the sun.

In colder months the dome is well-insulated thanks to a rubberized paint used to treat the outside. This also serves in the summer to deflect UV rays and therefore keep the interior cool. Sections of the dome's skin can be peeled back to provide the interior with ample ventilation thanks to the ocean breeze. This, along with the enormous bay window that gives onto the deck, also allows abundant natural light to enter. Another source of light are the round windows dotted about the domes surface, offering glimpses of the exterior.

The open plan interior is organized through light-weight, opaque screens, which divide the home into its different spaces, such as the kitchen and sleeping areas. A mezzanine has been used for the son's bedroom, providing him with a space of his own and intimacy when desired.

Aside from the minimal physical impact on the environment thanks to its ephemeral nature, the house also represents a significant reduction in energy consumption. Almost all of the electricity used by the home comes from solar panels, while the stove and refrigerator are fuelled by propane. The water supply comes from a tank located outside the property.

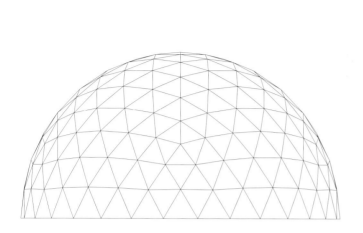

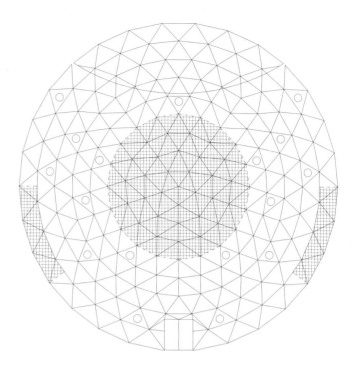

Shawn Hausman – Jessica Kimberley & Pacific Domes

Shubin + Donaldson Architects

Santa Barbara Riviera Residence

Santa Barbara, California

Photographs:
Ciro Coelho

Architects:
Shubin + Donaldson Architects
Principals:
Robin Donaldson, Russell Shubin
Project team:
Nils Hammerbeck, Daniel Webber,
Kelly Kish, Allison White, Josh Blumer,
Alan McLeod, David Van Hoy
Interiors:
Genie Gable Interior Design
Contractor:
Quillin Construction
Landscape:
Lane Goodkind

The clients wanted to take advantage of a classic Santa Barbara site on what is known as "The Riviera". Situated on a ridge, the near-perfect location commands a 270-degree view of the Pacific Ocean, a dramatic canyon, and the Santa Inez mountains.

The three-level home and two-car garage include open living/dining area, kitchen, master bedroom and bath, guest bedroom and bath, home gym, powder room, two home offices with office bath, outdoor dining area, outdoor lounge areas, lap pool, and 130 sqm (1400 sqft) of lower-level storage. Though not immediately obvious, this house embraces several characteristics of environmentally sustainable design. The basic design strategy is to site the house based on solar orientation, resulting in passive solar gains throughout the year. Photovoltaic power generates household electricity through a 2.8kw system (when power is not needed, it feeds back into the grid). A passive roof-top solar heating system provides for domestic hot water and a passive solar ground-level hot-water system is used to heat the pool. The natural flow of hot and cool air is fortified by the use of radiant hot-water floor heating and separate central air conditioning in the ceilings.

The architects re-used the existing foundation and caissons. During construction, the existing house was taken apart piece-by-piece, with all usable elements donated to Habitat for Humanity. Other energy-saving systems include double-pane windows, UV-resistant glass, ample insulation, and energy-efficient appliances. Deep exterior overhangs are designed to provide shade in the summer, and let in sun during the winter.

A dramatic glass canopy ceremoniously marks the entrance to the home, bisecting the ground-to-roof planes of glass that form sidelights and clerestories. Throughout the house, walls intersect with glass in a play of solidity and transparency. There is a certain efficiency of design in the layout, yet it provides all of the amenities so that the house looks and feels like a five-star private residential club.

A monumental feeling is emphasized by designing the house to constantly open up to the outdoors. A neutral color scheme complements the colors of nature that comprise the predominant palette. An infinity pool just outside the living room leads the eye to the ocean and the Channel Islands beyond. Four separate terraces surround the house, continuing the indoor/outdoor feeling and accessibility. Each room affords great vistas as well as stunning natural light throughout the day. Large windows create frames for nature. Floor-to-ceiling bookshelves complement the mahogany living room wall that houses an entertainment center. Set into the wall, and surrounded by floor-to-ceiling glass, it acts as an extension of the outdoors. Doorways in general – even in the limestone-clad bathrooms – are taller than usual and lead the eye upward to be rewarded by either natural light or a beautiful vista. Bedrooms and master bath look out to the ocean. The kitchen faces the hillside, emphasizing how the house maintains a connection with nature.

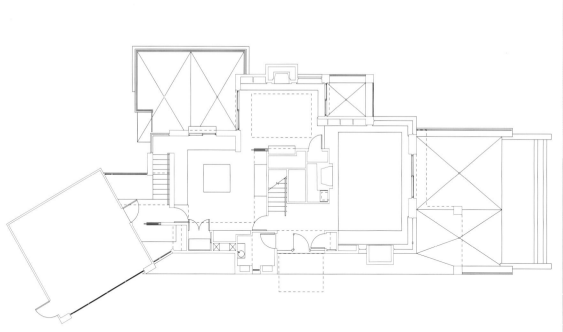

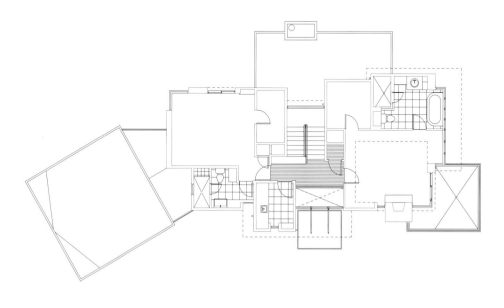

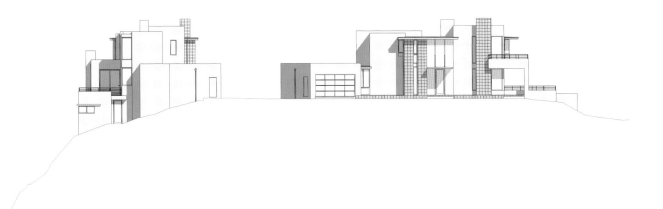

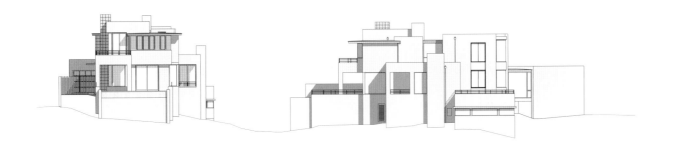

By taking up minimal space – what's absolutely necessary and no more – the house also takes up minimal resources. Although heating and cooling systems are in place, they are rarely used because of the solar orientation of the home and the natural ventilation.

Valentine Houses

Cambridge, Massachusetts

Photographs:
Erik Gould

Architect:
SINGLE speed DESIGN
John Hong, Jinhee Park, Andy Hong
Structural Engineer:
Sarkis Zerounian Associates
Landscape Contractor:
Boston Landscape, Inc.
Developer:
Azzam Development, Inc.

The site, in a dense Cambridge Massachusetts neighborhood, was previously a poorly maintained parking lot. Even before the construction commenced, water drainage issues created a problematic condition for the immediate area as well as the surrounding parcels. As the older city infrastructure was unable to sustain more runoff, a water management scheme to keep drainage onsite was devised: water retention catchments or 'green belts' line the edges of the site allowing landscape to flourish in these areas as well as filter the runoff. Permeable unit pavers, some of it salvaged from demolished 200 year-old Boston streetscapes, is placed over a gravel drainage layer to further allow water to penetrate into the subsurface rather than leave the site as runoff.

As the developer required the use of standard and tested building practices, the three town houses are constructed with 'off-the-shelf' materials chosen for their high recycled or renewable content. For example, the structural system is composed of composite structural members made with high recycled wood content, rather than more traditional solid wood framing. On the interior, renewable resources such as bamboo flooring rather than traditional hardwoods have been used.

During construction, careful planning to minimize waste such as non-recyclable gypsum wall board was put in place. Finally, an important aspect of sustainability that is often overlooked is the issue of labor. By using mainstream construction methods that required little additional training, the developer's existing construction crew was able to be employed throughout the project rather than be replaced with a specialized work force.

Double height spaces and strategic placing of glazing not only provides a sustainable lighting solution, but also promotes efficient heating and ventilation. Direct and indirect sunlight is brought deep into the building so that in many of the spaces, the need for powered light during daytime hours is effectively minimized. The double height voids also promote stack ventilation: in the summer, warm air rises to the top levels and is vented to the exterior, allowing cooler air to then be pulled in at lower levels. In the winter, low-emission, high-efficiency wood-burning stoves heat lower levels while interconnected open spaces bring this rising warmed air into the upper levels of the dwelling unit.

As well as being ecologically sound, the design of the Valentine Houses considers the social and cultural 'use' of the project along with its physical form. As a critique of the inward-looking 'winterized box', entry points for the building are not merely conceived as doorways, but as a sequence of paths and gathering spaces that negotiate public and private realms. Cantilevered garden-balconies and occupiable shared roof-planes become an architectural language for further urban developments in a city where density tends to overwhelm social open-space. Finally, the modest construction budget of the project allows the concept of sustainability to become more egalitarian and democratically available rather than restrictively expensive and customized.

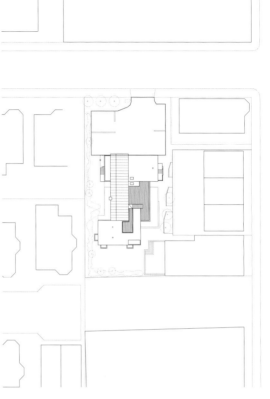

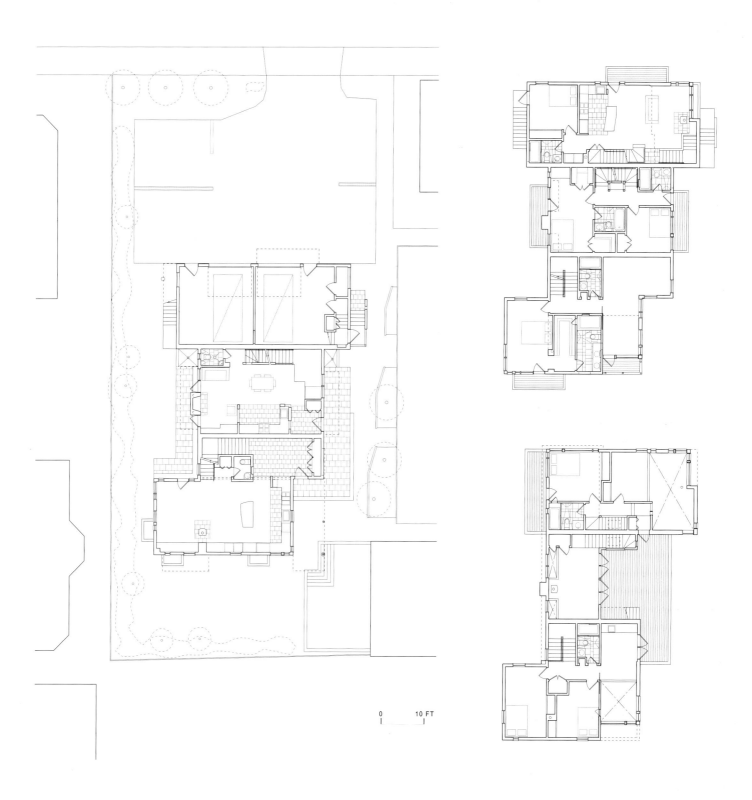

0 10 FT

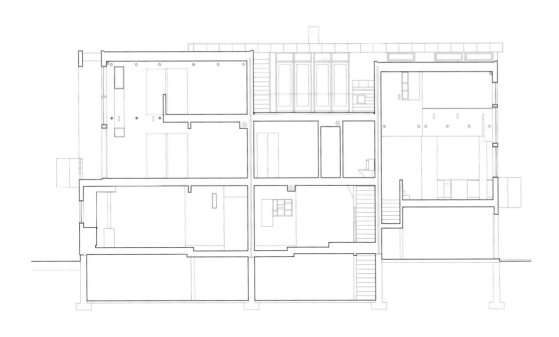

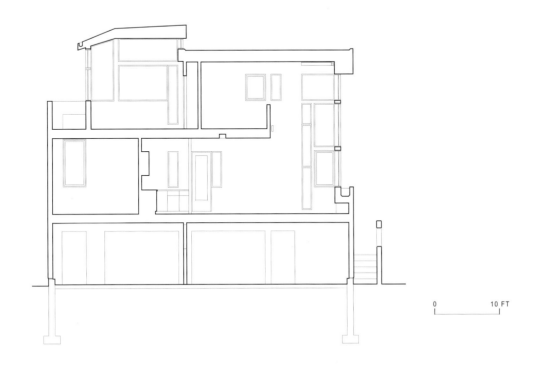

0   10 FT

As the developer required the use of standard and tested building practices, the three town houses are constructed with 'off-the-shelf' materials chosen for their high recycled or renewable content. For example, the structural system is composed of composite structural members made with high recycled wood content, rather than more traditional solid wood framing. On the interior, renewable resources such as bamboo flooring rather than traditional hardwoods have been used.

1. Reclaimed cobblestones from a local de-molished street used as pavers.
2. Flat-seamed copper clad fireplace and chimney.
3. Bamboo planter bed integrated into fa-cade of building.
4. Bamboo flooring from renewable sources.
5. Perforated balcony railing.
6. Rolling multifunctional dining table / kitchen cabinet.
7. Medicine cabinet light.

8. Galvanized steel fireplace box.
9. Permeable outdoor hardscape.
10. Painted roof deck guardrail.
11. "Found object" glass incorporated into clerestory window.
12. Lavastone countertops.
13. Cladding: beveled cedar, flat cedar, aluminium panel.
14. Permeable unit pavers in easement area.
15. Metal corners at exterior siding.
16. "Found object"borrowed light recess.

17. Glass mosaic and subway tile.
18. LC-copper standing seam cladding at balcony.
19. Recessed display niche.
20. Continuous slate, bath floor-wall.
21. Fabric light fixture.
22. Sliding office door.
23. Transition between walkway hardscape and softscape.
24. Pre-fab kitchen cabinets.
25. Hallway cd storage.
26. Granite boulder found on site made

into landscape feature.
27. Slate floor defining open kitchens
28. Wire-rope kit stair railing.
29. hovering stair landing.
30. Perforated aluminium at interior stair landing.
31. Powder room storage cabinets.
32. Running-bond prefab ply selving
33. Light as fluid material at stairhalls.
34. Runoff control planting beds.
35. Sandblasted plexi address plaques.

Marmol Radziner Prefab

Desert House

Desert Hot Springs, California

Photographs:
Benny Chan, Fotoworks

Marmol Radziner Prefab's prototype prefab home is oriented to best capture views of San Jacinto peak and the surrounding mountains. Located on a five-acre site in Desert Hot Springs, California, the house extends through the landscape with covered outdoor living areas, which double the 2000 square-foot interior spaces. A detached carport allows the owners to "leave the car behind" as they approach their home.

Designed for principal Leo Marmol and his wife Alisa Becket, the house employs four prefabricated house modules and six prefabricated deck modules. Sheltered living spaces blend the indoors with the outdoors, simultaneously extending and connecting the house to the north wing, which holds a guest house and studio space. By forming an "L", the home creates a protected environment that includes a pool and fire pit.

The home is built with prefabricated technologies in a factory out of three basics types of modules: interior modules comprising the living spaces, exterior modules defining covered outdoor living areas, and sunshade modules providing protection from the sun. Using steel framing, twelve foot wide modules extend up to sixty four feet in length. The modules employ different types of cladding, including metal, wood, or glass, or are simply left open to the surrounding landscape. The steel moment frame construction is sustainable and durable, while allowing for maximum flexibility in creating large expanses of open space and glass.

Just as the spaces of the home embrace nature, so too do the designs and methods of fabrication. The factory-made modules employ renewable and environmentally friendly materials. For example, the home is made from recycled steel rather than non-sustainable wood framing as the primary structural system. The home derives its electrical power from solar panels located on the roof above the bedroom. Deep overhangs shade the house from the harsh summer sun, and hidden pockets hold window shades that provide additional protection from the sun. In colder months, concrete floors absorb solar energy during the day and release the stored heat at night, helping to make the home sustainable. To increase insulation from the extensive fenestration, the home uses triple-pane, low-e, argon-filled insulating glass for the windows and glass doors. Because factory-construction provides greater precision in cutting materials and increases the ability to save and reuse excess material, the construction of the home created create significantly less waste than a home built on site.

Seeking to compliment the modern aesthetic of the architecture and the rustic beauty of the desert surroundings, the interior design reflects great esteem for nature and obscures distinctions between indoor and outdoor living spaces. By combining vintage, contemporary, and custom pieces, the home has a feel of understated elegance that highlights a connection to the earth.

1. Master bedroom
2. Hall
3. Entry
4. Kitchen
5. Bath
6. Dining
7. Living
8. Outdoor living
9. Pool
10. Guest bedroom
11. Studio
12. Deck

The modules were fabricated in the factory and shipped to the site including many pre-installed finishes, such as the custom wood cabinets and polished concrete floors. The modules were then craned on to the foundation, with minimal work remaining to complete the installation. As a prototype home, this house provided valuable design, fabrication, and installation lessons for the development of the Marmol Radziner Prefab's new line of modern prefab homes.

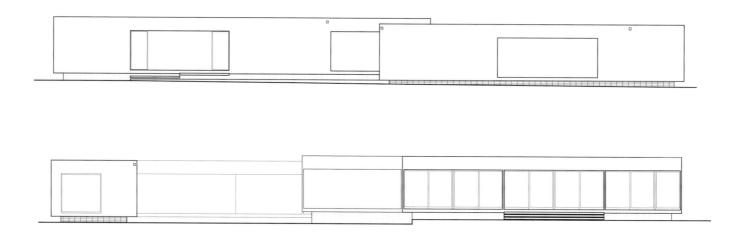

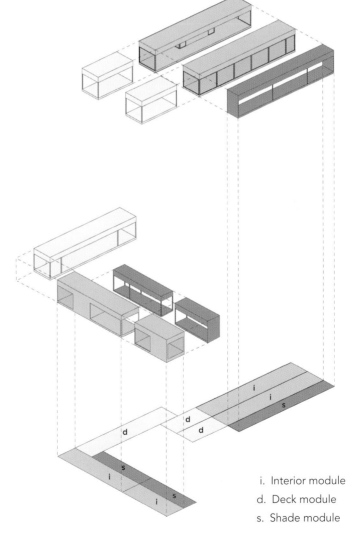

i. Interior module
d. Deck module
s. Shade module

Wilkinson Residence

Portland , Oregon

Photographs:
Cameron Neilson, Meredith Brower,
Randy Calvert

The designs of Portland architect Robert Oshatz defy categorization and boggle the imagination. This wildly creative wave-shaped house with continuous walls of glass, a D-shaped pivotal glass door entryway, and a copper exterior is yet another example of his style, which is at once highly innovative, functional and ecologically sound.

This house's location on a flag lot with a fast sloping grade provided the opportunity to bring the main level into the tree canopy, thereby evoking the feeling of living in a tree house. A lover of music, the client wanted a house that not only became a part of the natural landscape but also addressed the flow of music. The spaces of the house are difficult to grasp as they flow inside and out. One has to actually stroll through the house to capture its complexities and its connection to the exterior. This is achieved through the use of a natural wood ceiling floating on curving laminated wood beams, which pass through a generous glass wall, which in turn wraps around the main living room.

The house is conceived as a series of horizontal planes that terrace along the edge of a south-facing hill above a creek. The arrangement of the main living space and lower bedroom level, which wrap along the hill's crest, is a response to the topography, solar orientations and views beyond. From the entry courtyard, the low profile of the house and selective openings through the façade allow for a playful 'hide and reveal' of the landscape without dominating the site. This project is rooted in the Utopian modernist tradition of blending ambiguity between interior and exterior space. In the primary living spaces, the horizontal planes of the floor and roof surfaces extend beyond large openings of glass. The interior is characterized by multiple planes of light entering the house at a variety of levels.

Oshatz has addressed ecological questions in a number of different ways. Firstly, there is no air conditioning in the house, as it has been designed to provide ample cross ventilation. In particular, fresh air that has been shaded by the cantilever floor soffit of the living room enters the interior through vents in the toe space of the living room cabinet, which stands against the east glazing wall. It then creates a draft that draws the warm interior air out through the clerestory windows above the kitchen. There is also a light well above the lower floor hallway that draws cool air from the partially subterranean lower floor up to the main floor. For the colder months of the year the house is installed with radiant floor heating, which is powered by a high-efficiency natural gas water heater.

Reducing the house's environmental impact was also a major issue in the construction process. The finish wood, framing lumber, and cabinet woods came from certified sustainable forest, where possible, toxic chemicals were not used in the manufacturing of materials or on the construction site, and finally, waste material during construction was separated and brought to a recycling center.

Cameron Neilson

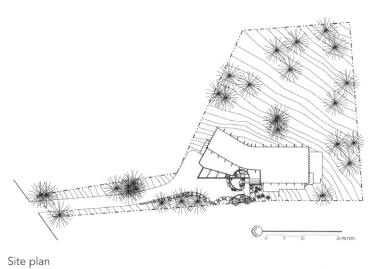

Site plan

Meredith Brower

Meredith Brower

Cameron Neilson

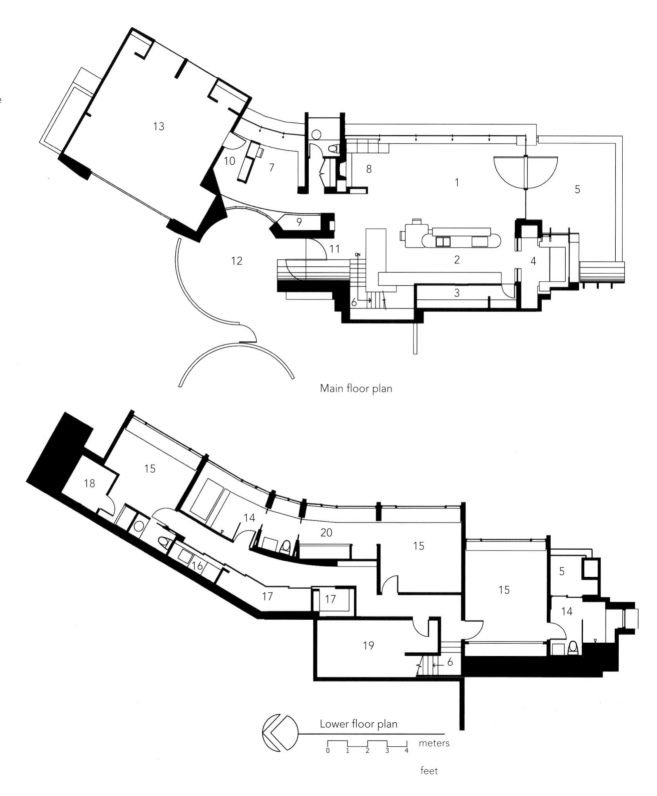

1. Living/dining
2. Kitchen
3. Pantry
4. Meditation
5. Deck
6. Stairs
7. Study
8. Fireplace alcove
9. Light well
10. Service entry
11. Entry
12. Courtyard
13. Garage
14. Bathroom
15. Bedroom
16. Laundry
17. Storage
18. Dark room
19. Wine cellar
20. Dressing

Main floor plan

Lower floor plan

meters

0 1 2 3 4

feet

The house is conceived as a series of horizontal planes that terrace along the edge of a south-facing hill above a creek. From the entry courtyard, the low profile of the house and selective openings through the façade allow for a playful 'hide and reveal' of the landscape without dominating the site. This project is rooted in the Utopian modernist tradition of blending ambiguity between interior and exterior space.

Randy Calvert

Cameron Neilson

Cameron Neilson

Randy Calvert

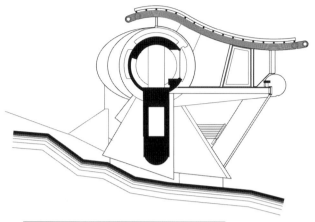
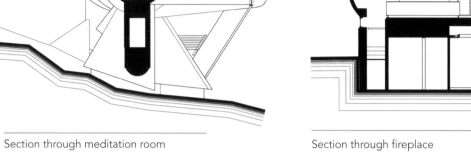

Section through meditation room

Section through fireplace

Cameron Neilson

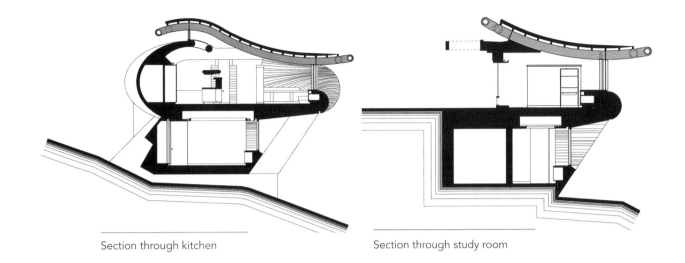

Section through kitchen

Section through study room

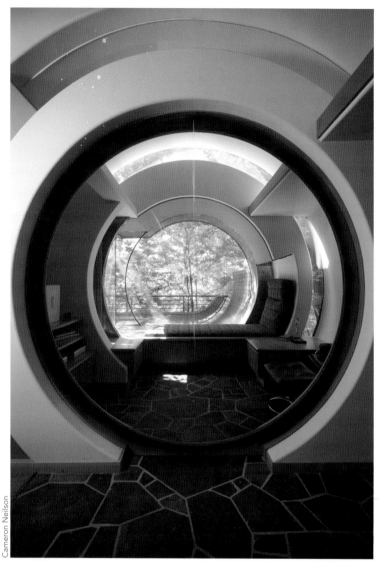

Cameron Neilson

Cameron Neilson

Cameron Neilson

Cameron Neilson

The Trojan Goat

Washington, D.C.

Photographs:
Prakash Patel

The Solar Decathlon, a competition organized by the U.S. Department of Energy and the National Renewable Energy Laboratory, brought together fourteen universities from across the country to compete in ten events focused on energy-efficient house design. The purpose of the competition was to encourage innovation in renewable energy by requiring entrants to design and build an 800 square foot house powered entirely by photovoltaic solar panels.

Students at the University of Virginia spent countless hours designing, debating and building their entry, named the "Trojan Goat." The name refers to both the unfolding wooden exterior skin (similar to the wooden Trojan Horse of ancient mythology), and the highly flexible design. Goats are the most adaptable of mammals, and can be found in almost all areas of the world. Like a goat, the house is climate-responsive and can adapt to a variety of weather conditions. Passive solar design, as well as highly efficient mechanical, electrical and plumbing systems, are essential components of the design. Powered entirely by a photovoltaic array, the house employs an integrated energy storage system for use at night or on rainy days, and a computer-controlled system to optimize the distribution of power. Windows and skylights are strategically placed to maximize natural ventilation and daylighting. Mechanically controlled louvers can be adjusted to minimize or maximize heat gain. A sun space provides an adaptable indoor/outdoor room that utilizes thermal mass to store heat, which is distributed at night to adjacent interior spaces.

Goats are also well known for turning others waste into food. Inspired by this, the team attempted to creatively reuse discarded materials – reclaiming waste products before they entered a landfill or scrap yard. Shipping palettes, for example, were used for the louvers, while the exterior boasts reclaimed copper cladding. Where reclaimed materials were not appropriate or available, the team carefully selected the new materials, to minimize the impact of the building on the environment.

Inside, the furniture and cabinetry was designed and built from sustainably forested lumber, which was used for most of the interior finishes. The team also designed the surrounding landscape, including a gray water collection/filtration system, green roof, planters, decks, and garden.

To improve the light conditions a domestic scale version of an emerging technology was assembled that provides natural daylight at locations far from a window. A mirror dish on the roof of the house tracks the sun, and concentrates it into a polished glass fiber cable to "deliver" the natural light directly into the house's bathroom and entry hall.

This house is both poetic and rational and shows that creating an ecological home is not just about sticking a photovoltaic panel on the roof.

The Trojan Goat was designed and built by a team of over 100 graduate and undergraduate students at the University of Virginia in Charlottesville, Virginia. The team of architecture, engineering, landscape architecture, planning, environmental science, economics and business students won the architecture and energy balance competitions in the 2002 Solar Decathlon. Architecture professor John Quale and engineering professor Paxton Marshall led the team. For more information about the Trojan Goat, see the teams website: www.faculty.virginia.edu/solarhome/

Quale and Marshall now run a program at UVA called ecoMOD, focused on sustainable, affordable and prefabricated housing for affordable housing organizations. The website is www.ecomod.virginia.edu

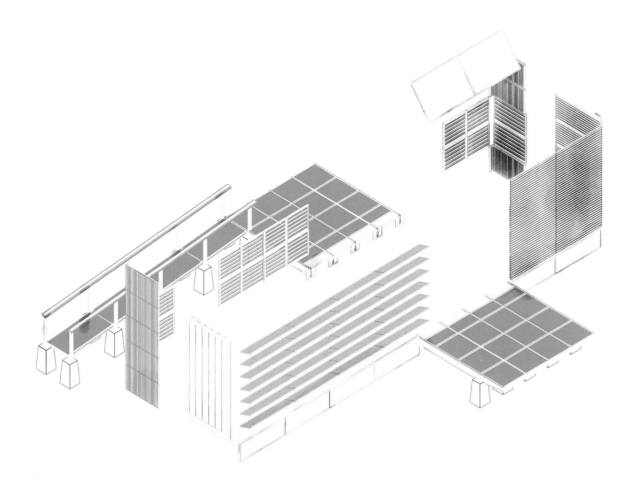

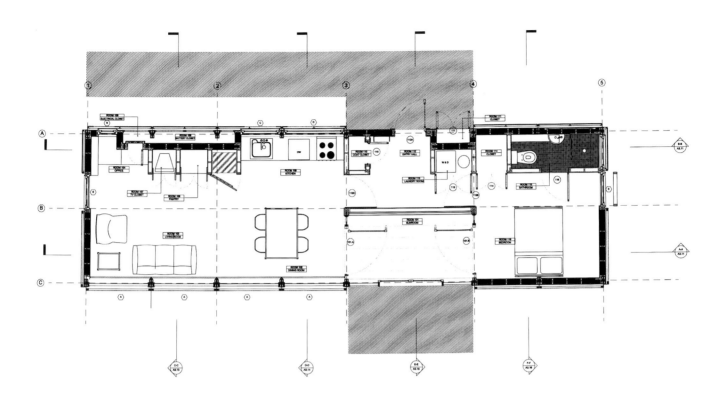

Inside, the furniture and cabinetry was designed and built from sustainably forested lumber, which was used for most of the interior finishes. The team also designed the surrounding landscape, including a gray water collection/filtration system, green roof, planters, decks, and garden.

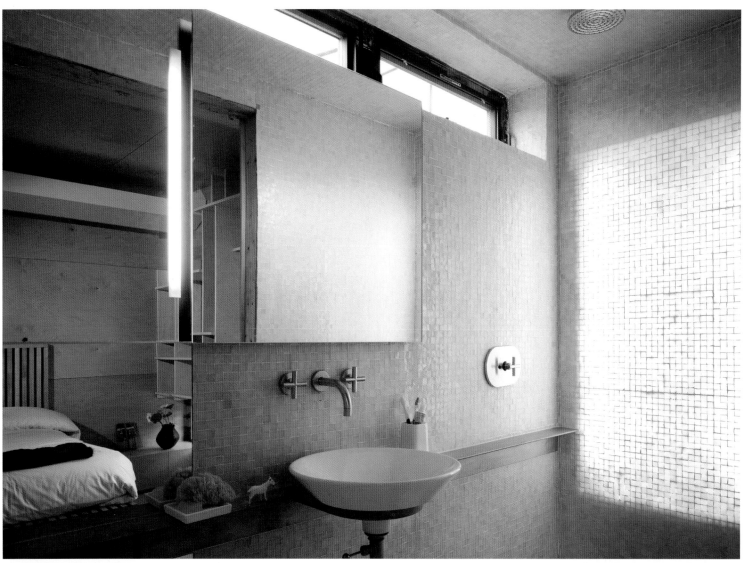

Factor 10 House

Chicago, Illinois

Photographs:
Doug Snower

Factor 10 House was an entry for a competition organized by the City of Chicago Departments of Environment and Housing, which invited architects to come up with designs for homes that incorporate innovative, energy efficient technologies and sustainable building practices. Using the four strategies of size reduction, improved efficiency, extended life span and impact reduction, Factor 10 House strives to reduce life-cycle environmental impacts by a factor of 10 compared to the average home built in America today.

Factor 10's base design is a straightforward response to four primary considerations: a narrow city site with adjacent buildings, a modular design, an open 115 sqm (1234 sqft) floor plan, and a solar chimney incorporated into the stairwell of the home. Each addresses the critical efficiencies of use of materials and energy consumption.

Materials were selected for their extended life spans and initial production impact. Recycled materials were incorporated wherever possible. The modular design works within industry's dimensional constraints, minimizing waste of materials and allowing off-site assembly. The open floor plan enhances cross ventilation and the careful placement of windows maximizes reflected light into the interior of the home, reducing glare.

The solar chimney, a key element of the design, is located in the center of the home and houses the stairs. By carefully controlling light through a south-facing clerestory window, it brings light to the core of the house reducing the need for artificial lighting. Augmented by a whole-house fan, the shaft was designed to pull warm air up and out of the house in the summer, and push warm air down in the winter. A wall of full water bottles acts as a heat sink in the winter. Energy consumption is minimized by the promotion of natural ventilation—eliminating the reliance on air-conditioning—maximizing insulation, use of a gas-fired boiler with perimeter baseboard heat and the aid of the bottle wall heat sink.

The first floor level is raised to match neighboring houses on the street. A basement is incorporated into the design, allowing for future living space expansion. The basement has sufficient natural light and ventilation for residential occupancy. It houses the washer and dryer, gas-fired boiler, and water heater, allowing the other two floors to enjoy a more unencumbered plan. A no-maintenance sedum green roof on the house minimizes storm water runoff, making the entire site permeable.

Architects:
EHDD Architecture
Marc L'Italien, Design principal
Marjorie Brownstein, Project manager
Susan Hagerty, Project architect
Scott Shell, Green technology specialist
Structural engineer:
Klein & Hoffman
Josh Dortzbach, Project engineer
Mechanical/electrical/plumbing engineers:
Mechanical Services Associates Corp.
Bob Larsen, Project engineer
HERS Consultant:
Renacer Westside Community Network, Inc.
Architectural specifications consultant:
ArchiTech Consulting
General contractor:
Telion Contracting Corp.
Konstantinos (Gus) Chaniotakis
Developer:
Neighborhood Housing Services of Chicago, Annette Conti
Client/Owner:
City of Chicago Department of Environment, N. Marcia Jimenez, Commissioner

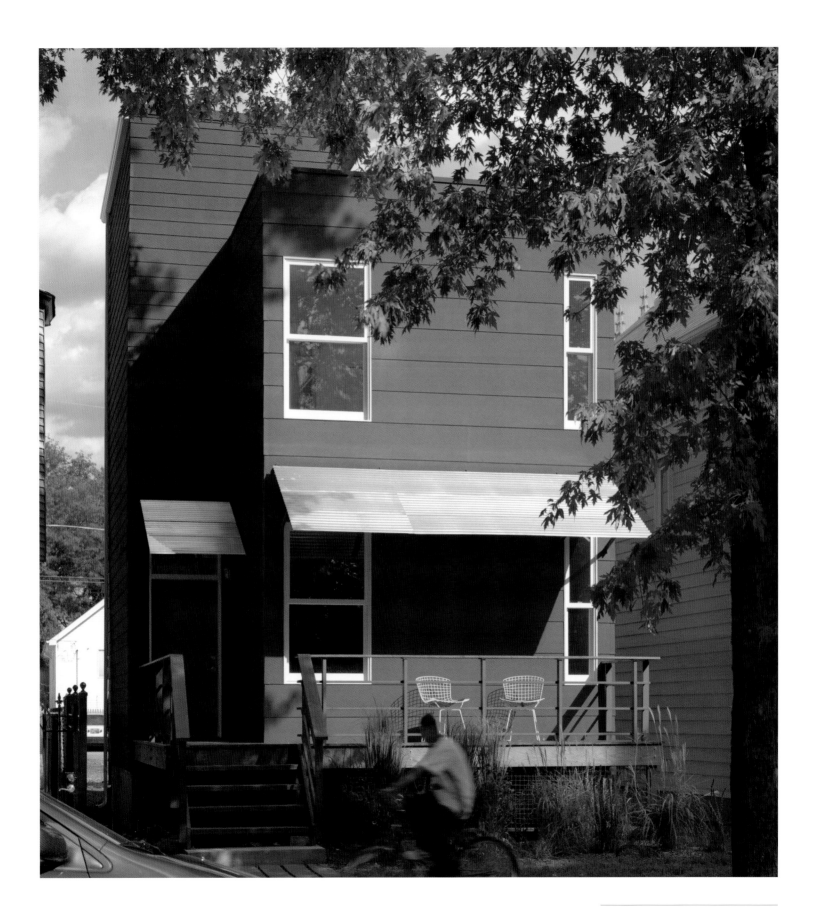

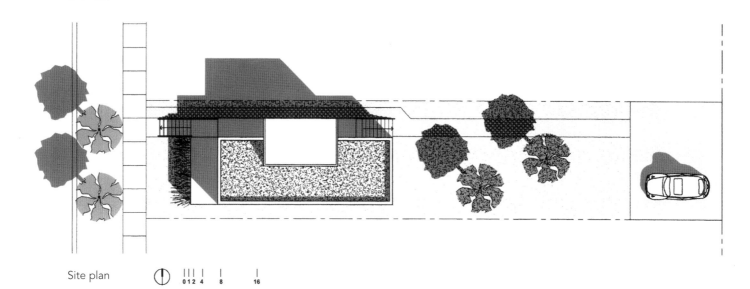

Site plan ⊕ ||| | | | 0 1 2 4 8 16

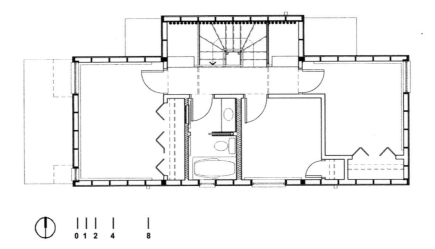

First floor plan

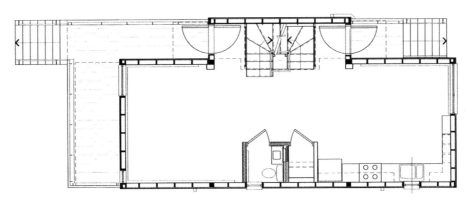

Ground floor plan

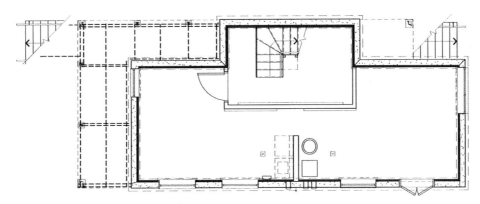

Basement plan

The Factor 10 house maximizes efficiency, uses sustainable building materials, is designed with modular units to reduce material waste, is sited to maximize naturallight and heat resources. The goal is to reduce the building's impact by a factor of ten compared to an average home.

Green roof system

Excelent insulation, curbs water run-off, prevents city heat build-up, discharges oxygen, looks great.

Daylighting

Large clestory windows work in tandem with the open stair and glass transoms to bring natural light through the house.

Passive heating / cooling system

Solar chimney: Whole house fan pulls air through the house and evacuates hot air out. Ceiling fan at solar chimney circulates warm air down in winter.
Bottle wall: Wall of drinking water bottles acts as a heat sink in winter colleting the sun's heat by the day and slowly emmiting the heat during the night.
Natural ventilation: Trasom windows at all second floor doors to facilitate natural air movement.

Sustainable materials

Exterior wall construction:
    cement board panel siding
    1/2" rigid insulation
    5/8" gypsum board
    2x6 certified wood framing
    blown-in celulose insulation
    5/8" gypsum board
High Fly Ash concrete in basement. Uses less intensive manufacturing process and creates fewer global warming gasses than regular concrete. This by-product of coal-fired power plants generaly ends up in landfills. adding it to concrete in high volumes creates a stronger more durable product that reduces environmental impact.

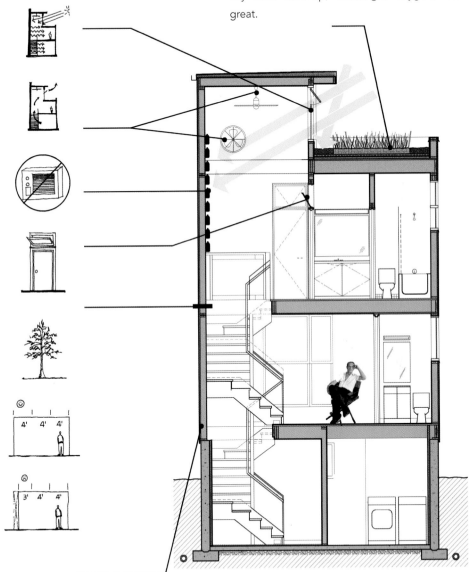

Waste-less layout

All wood framing at 2'-0" o.c.
Plan layout uses 2'-0" module to minimize material waste.

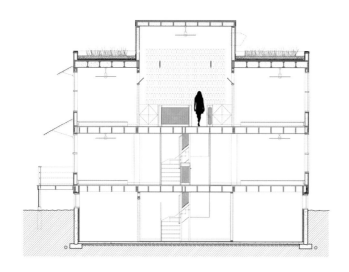

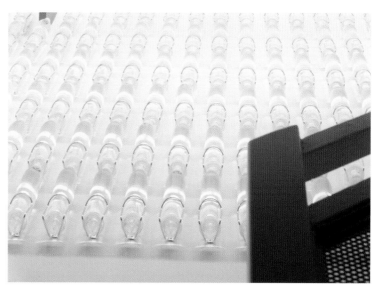

Seatrain House

Los Angeles, California

Photographs:
Undine Pröhl

Design Team:
Principal: Jennifer Siegal
Senior Designer: Kelly Bair
Assistant: Andrew Todd
Creative Director &
General Contractor:
Richard Carlson
Interior Design:
Arkkit Forms / David Mocarski
Landscape Design:
James Stone
Waterscape Design:
Jim thompson
Water Features:
Liquid Works / Rik Jones
Steel Fabrication:
Steel Man / Don Griggs
Glass Fabrication:
Penguin Construction /
Gadie Aharoni
Artist:
Phillip Slagter

This 3000 square foot residence is situated in a 300-loft live-and-work artist community by the Brewery. Industrial and traditional materials are playfully combined, using storage containers and steel found on-site in downtown LA.

Large panels of glass throughout the house open up the space, allowing natural light to pour in, connecting it to the rest of the community. The project has been a collaborative experiment between the client and the builders, where creative and structural decisions were made as the house was being constructed.

This home literally grows up from the land around it, engaging with and incorporating the industrial history of downtown LA by using found-on-site materials. Grain trailers are transformed into a koi fishpond and a lap pool. The large storage containers are used to create and separate the dwelling spaces within the house. Each storage container has its own individual function, one is the entertainment and library area, another is a dining room and office space overlooking the garden below, another serves as the bathroom and laundry room and yet another is the master bedroom, a visually dramatic protruding volume that wraps around the upper part of the house. This unfussy space allows for the dynamic interplay of materials and forms, the contrast of corrugated metals, industrial containers and exposed wooden beams all highlighted with warm, calm green hues.

All of the containers used in the house have been altered in surprising ways. Some have been severed into separate pieces, others have been added onto, layered or wrapped, showing the myriad design possibilities in repurposing these materials. There are wrapped design elements throughout the house including a 12-foot high steel plate fence that wraps around the entire site. It lifts up at one point, stretching to become a canopy that shades the entrance, creating the feeling that the ground tilts upward. Here, recycled materials are not just practical and cost effective; they create a unique, dramatic architectural vocabulary. Combined with steel and glass, the result is sculptural, open and LA modern, creating an oasis without disguising the industrial source of inspiration.

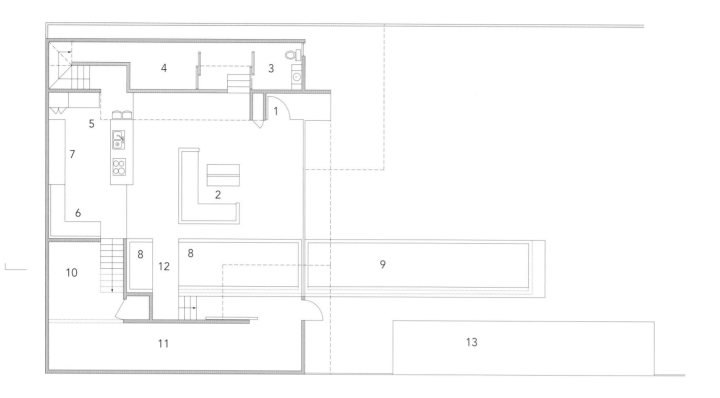

Ground floor plan

1. Entry
2. Living room
3. Guest bath
4. Utility and laundry
5. Kitchen
6. Lounge
7. Bar
8. Interior Koi pond
9. Lap pool
10. Library
11. Media room
12. Foot bridge
13. Guest house

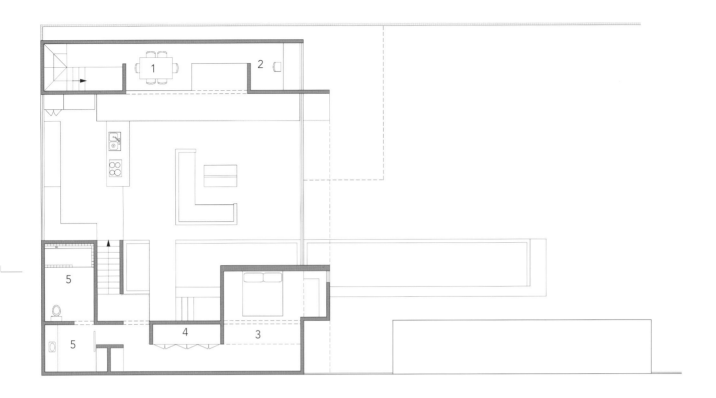

First floor plan

1. Dining room
2. Office
3. Master bedroom
4. Closet
5. Master bathroom

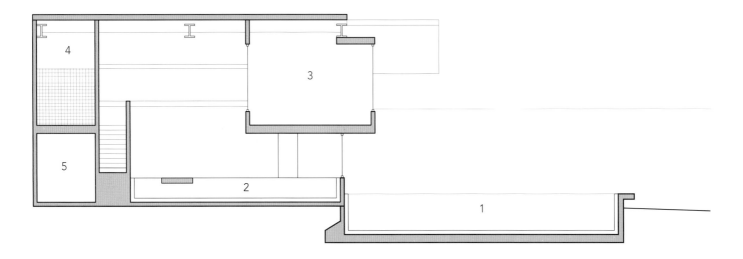

Section AA

1. Lap pool
2. Interior Koi pond
3. Master bedroom
4. Master bathroom
5. Library

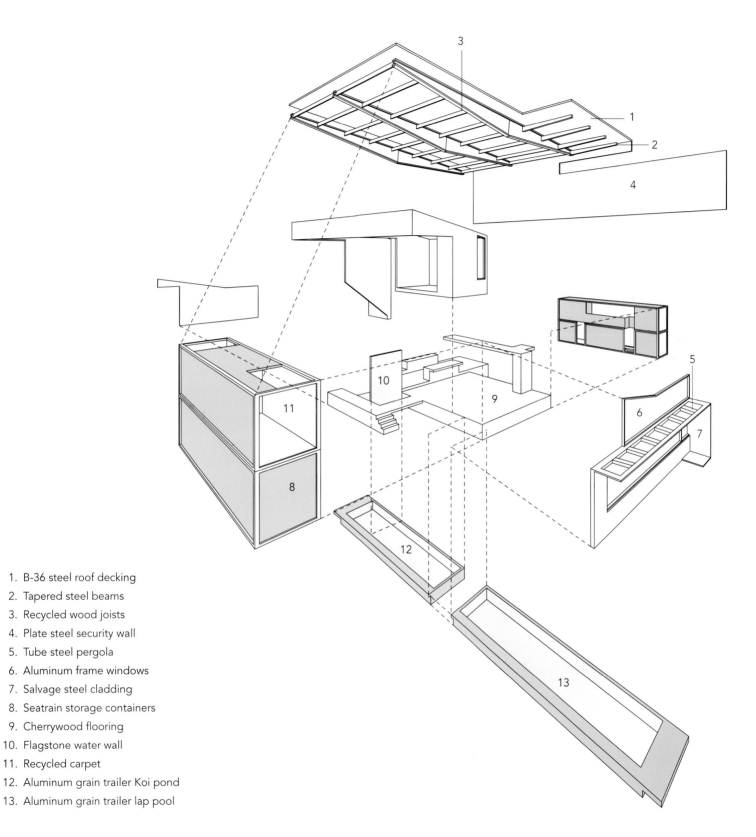

1. B-36 steel roof decking
2. Tapered steel beams
3. Recycled wood joists
4. Plate steel security wall
5. Tube steel pergola
6. Aluminum frame windows
7. Salvage steel cladding
8. Seatrain storage containers
9. Cherrywood flooring
10. Flagstone water wall
11. Recycled carpet
12. Aluminum grain trailer Koi pond
13. Aluminum grain trailer lap pool

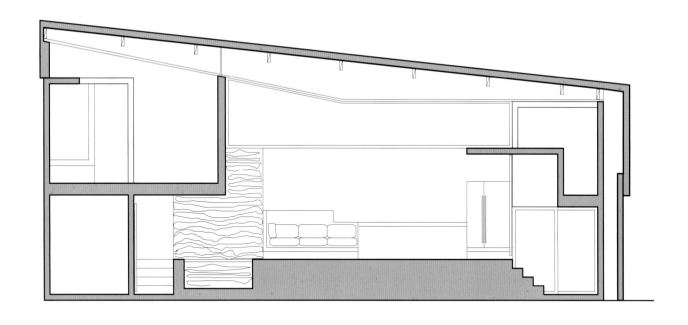

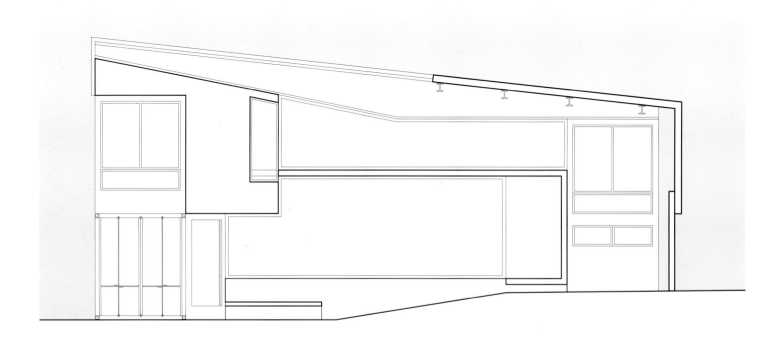

Bartlit Residence

Castle Pines, Colorado

Photographs:
Hester+Hardaway

Since the clients expressed the desire for a "seamless indoor outdoor connection to take advantage of the expansive views," the design solution took its cues from the natural land formations on the site. What appears to be a series of low granite riparian walls course down the hill and form the base of the house. Superimposed on this heavy base are light exposed steel and glass "pavilions" with sloping copper roofs that catch the sun and frame the views while sheltering the glass from rain and snow. The house is cut into the hillside and two of the guest rooms are located under a sod roof to minimize the appearance of the house from the street and to allow some of the west facing rooms to open out to the existing grade.

A dialogue is created between heavy stone, light steel and glass that roots the house firmly in the land and blurs the division between inside and out. The dialogue continues throughout the house in a play of light, opacity, permanence and changing vistas. To reinforce the relationship between indoors and out, a series of carefully detailed openings – courtyards, atriums and windows – provide glimpses of the surroundings. This connection culminates in an outdoor arbor with stone floors that flow from the gallery out through large glass pocket doors.

The clients envisioned "a house that feels like it was built 200 years ago by a forward thinking architect." A careful selection of local granite and sandstone give the home the "of the earth" look the owner requested. Specific materials were selected for their character, patina and enduring nature. The native Empire, Gunnison granite and Colorado sandstone move easily from exterior to interior, from floors to walls.

The design process was able to address the project's specific challenges through an innovative use of stone. Passive solar heating provides winter heat through internal granite walls providing thermal mass at both atriums. All pavilion rooms (living, dining, master and exercise) have southern solar exposure coupled with massive walls. Radiant heat exists in concert with forced air-heating/cooling in the pavilions.

To preserve the existing vegetation and rock formations of the cliffside, the site was carefully chosen to minimize the appearance of the house from the street side and maximize the views to the front range of the Rocky Mountains. Rustic granite walls anchored by boulders burrow into the hillside, recalling an overgrown ruin and keeping a low profile to the street.

1 - Entry   2 - Gallery   3 - Kitchen / Family   4 - Living
5 - Arbor   6 - Solarium

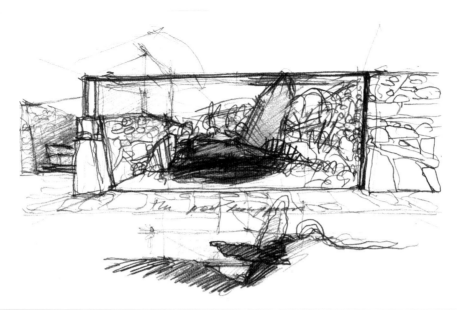

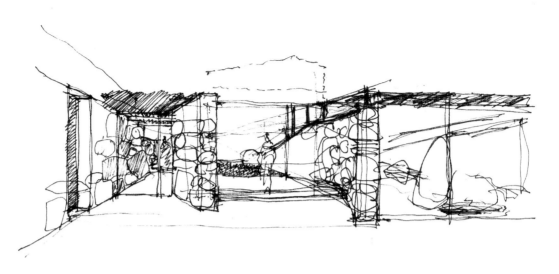

Loft and Studio – Dog Team Too

San Antonio, Texas

Photographs:
Hester + Hardaway

The original exterior openings of this loft apartment, a jumble of remodeled store fronts, have been removed and replaced with cement infill panels and frosted upper glass windows, to create light filled spaces while maintaining privacy and security in this inner city neighborhood.

The overall layout is similar to an industrial hacienda. The compound is entered via the old alley, now the "outdoor entry hall," between the living and working structures and terminates at the new courtyard. New walls, planting and a raised "water trough" pool create an oasis-like setting in this hot industrial area. The living and working areas open directly to the courtyard. A third structure, a small storage building with walls removed, became the courtyard pavilion.

The original wood roof structure of the living loft, destroyed by a fire, was replaced with a "light steel" north-facing saw-tooth design, which stabilized the free standing brick walls, while also bringing a generous amount of natural light into the living area. The light steel and smooth plywood design contrasts with the strongly textured wood structure of the work area.

The loft space consists of a rectangular open plan living area with glass doors to the courtyard and ceramic coated windows placed high along the outside walls to the north and east. The windows keep out the distraction of traffic and passing pedestrians, while letting in soft, diffused natural light.

At the south end, an existing steel room became the dining alcove. The ceiling has exposed wood trusses and a saw-tooth structure with north-facing clerestory windows that from certain angles display one continuous band of blue sky, which provides more natural light for the large space.

The kitchen, with custom-made steel cabinets and concrete countertops, takes up the southeast corner of the living area, and a guest bathroom is tucked conveniently off to the side. The bedroom and private areas at the north end are separated from the main space by a set of large hanging rolling doors veneered with black chalkboard.

Across the courtyard the working studio is used for photo shoots and other creative projects. The open plan is broken only by a darkroom built out from a corner; its walls also veneered in black chalkboard to provide a surface for notes and drawings. Both living and working spaces retain the rugged character of the original industrial buildings. By paring down the interior finishes and exposing structural elements, the spaces acquire a modern sensibility that reflects the lifestyle and accommodates the work of the owner.

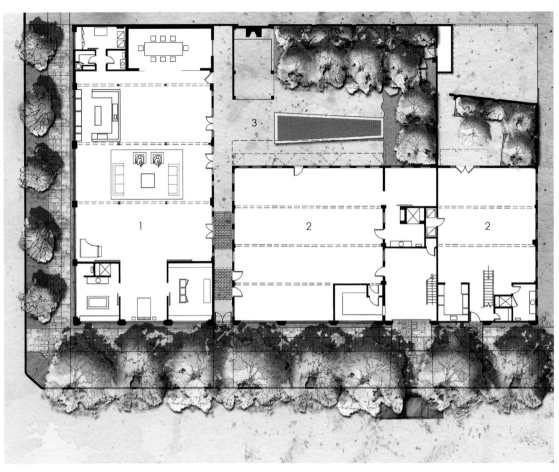

1 - Living Loft   2 - Studio   3 - Pool Court

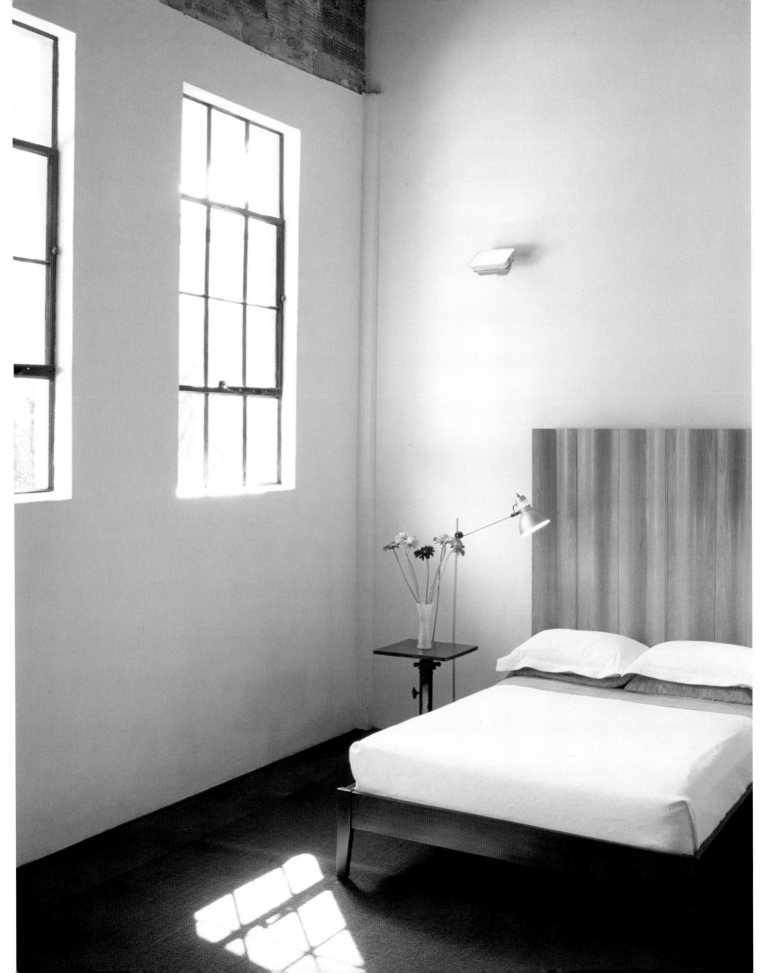

Courtyard House

Los Angeles, California

Photographs:
Marla Aufmuth, Thomas Robertson,
Nana Doors

Design team:
Ripple Design.
Thomas Robertson, principal
Project Team:
Thomas Robertson, John Eckholm,
Paul Waldron, Guy Kraus, Eric Bono
General contractor:
Ernesto Alonzo, Alonzo Construction
Concrete:
Macias Construction
Retractable door systems:
Nana
Custom cabinetry:
Ripple Design
Steel fabrication:
Christer Lannerholm + Alumina Design
Powder coating:
Tortoise Industries
Hanging sculpture:
Mary Brogger

This courtyard house, designed by American designer Thomas Robertson, integrates a sense of being in a city with that of feeling at home, two seemingly contradictory experiences. The urban experience is filtered into the house while an intimate sense of privacy is preserved. A very awkward hillside lot with a significant height differential in a very "quaint" neighborhood serves as the site for this complicated yet very intriguing structure. The owner requested a house that resembled a loft, while offering lots of nooks and crannies for art and diverse collections. It also needed to fit into its surroundings and the context of its neighborhood.

Proceeding through the house, the courtyard reveals itself as a kind of plaza on a micro-urban scale ideal for relaxing or entertaining. The rest of the program for the house revolves around this central space. The design makes full use of passive strategies of climatic control, thereby offering financial benefits to the client and a reduced ecological footprint to the community. Just one example of this is the courtyard doors. When opened, the outside becomes the inside of the house. Various combinations of these doors opened and closed can regulate comfort via breezes and heat gain as well as diverse social interactions.

Designing this type of home requires careful attention to detail and a great dedication to thoroughly thinking things through. The way in which the house is nestled into the hillside; the thickening of specific walls and ceilings; the exploitation of dense or reflective materials; all these utilize thermal mass to modulate heat gain and eliminate the need for air conditioning systems. Furthermore, the orientation of the house maximizes the possibilities for passive cooling and heating.

Technological systems play a significant role in the house. Where systems are utilized, they are highly efficient. Solar cells heat water and create electrical energy. In fact, this house creates all of its own power, feeding its surpluses back into the city grid.

The emphasis here is that the choice to reduce the ecological footprint can start in the home. Deciding to use local craftsmen and materials means fewer resources are necessary or wasted. Many of the materials are sustainably forested, long-lasting and break down easily in landfills. The ultimate choice is to improve the quality of life in order to reduce the perceived need - especially in a city like Los Angeles - to wander so frequently from home.

Marla Aufmuth

Marla Aufmuth

Thomas Robertson

Marla Aufmuth

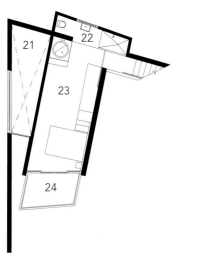

Second floor plan

1. Mechanical room
2. Storage
3. Lower courtyard
4. Garage
5. Study
6. Storage
7. Darkroom
8. Living room
9. Foyer
10. Bathroom 1
11. Balcony
12. Dining nook

13. Breakfast nook
14. Kitchen
15. Den
16. Laundry
17. Hall
18. Bathroom 2
19. Bedroom 1
20. Upper courtyard
21. Open to below
22. Bathroom 3
23. Bedroom 2
24. Balcony

First floor plan

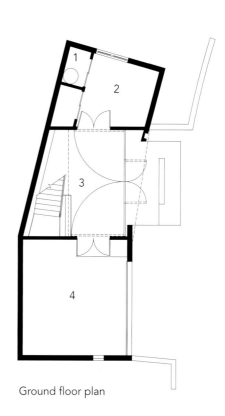

Ground floor plan

Nana Doors

Designing this type of home requires careful attention to detail and a great dedication to thoroughly thinking things through. The way in which the house is nestled into the hillside; the thickening of specific walls and ceilings; the exploitation of dense or reflective materials; all these utilize thermal mass to modulate heat gain and eliminate the need for air conditioning systems. Furthermore, the orientation of the house maximizes the possibilities for passive cooling and heating.

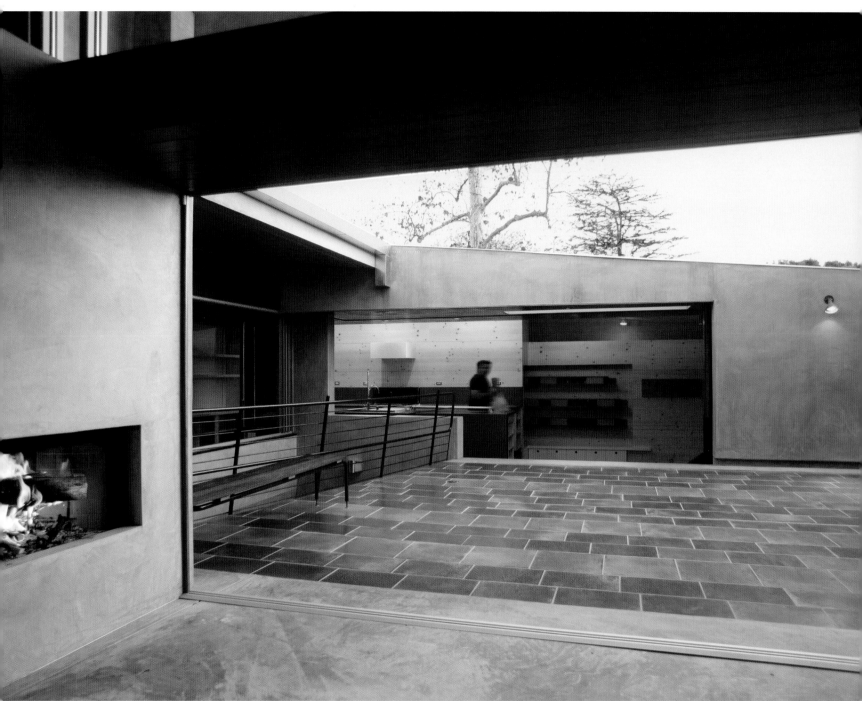

Marla Aufmuth

Nana Doors

Marla Aufmuth

Marla Aufmuth

The Snee-Oosh Cabin

Snee Oosh, Washington

Photographs:
Contributed by Zero Plus Architects

Like a rabbit warming itself in the sun, the Snee-oosh Cabin sits in the underbrush, perched on a low bank at the waters edge near Deception Pass on the Swinomish Indian reservation. Intended as a getaway from the increasingly urban Seattle landscape, it was conceived as a covered platform in the trees, protected but closely connected to the surrounding marine forest and expansive bay with its dramatic currents and tides. In a site where the spirit of place is so compelling, dissolving the barriers between inside and out became a prime motivation. Building with reverence and care not to destroy the special qualities of the site required careful placement and a building system that was light and flexible, using the smallest footprint possible.

The construction borrows from "reservation vernacular" with exposed strand board, modular pieces, inexpensive Hardie sheets and rolled roofing. The result is a "lean to" style building, which constitutes a new, modern reservation architecture.

Eight concrete disks narrowly avoid the 30 m (100 ft) tall fir trees and their roots while isolating the impact of the house on the complex top soil layer to ensure continued tree health. A steel skeleton bolted to these eight disks supports and braces a hanging wooden belly and an oversized foam panel roof. The foam panels are structural and are made from 20 cm (8 in) of expanded polystyrene sand-wiched by two layers of oriented strand board. The steel skeleton collects both the lateral and gravity loads and delivers them to the eight disks, leaving the platform free of lateral concerns, and allows the trusses to reach across the platform and nearly float towards the south. All of these pieces were carefully designed to work together structurally, be prefabricated off site, and be fitted together like a delicate puzzle or the intricate pieces of an insect.

Large monitors poke out of the roof and draw light from above through the fir canopy, providing strong passive ventilation that is augmented by a giant industrial ceiling fan, which can be used to either slowly adjust heat stratification or quickly make an air change. The hanging wooden belly is heavily insulated with just a few carefully placed windows and the foam roof work to protect the tiny, energy-efficient sleeping rooms. These contrast with the "camp like" living spaces of the platform, which are protected from the weather by a transparent glass skin that joins the living spaces with the surrounding dense brush. The glazing system, a combination of sealant and vertical steel flat bars that mimic the vertical rhythm of the surrounding trees, wraps around the platform.

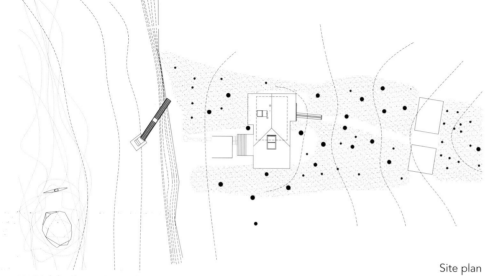

Site plan

1. Entry ramp
2. Entry deck
3. Living
4. Kitchen
5. Shower
6. Toilet
7. Utility
8. Hang deck
9. Court
10. Sleep 1
11. Sleep 2
12. Loft

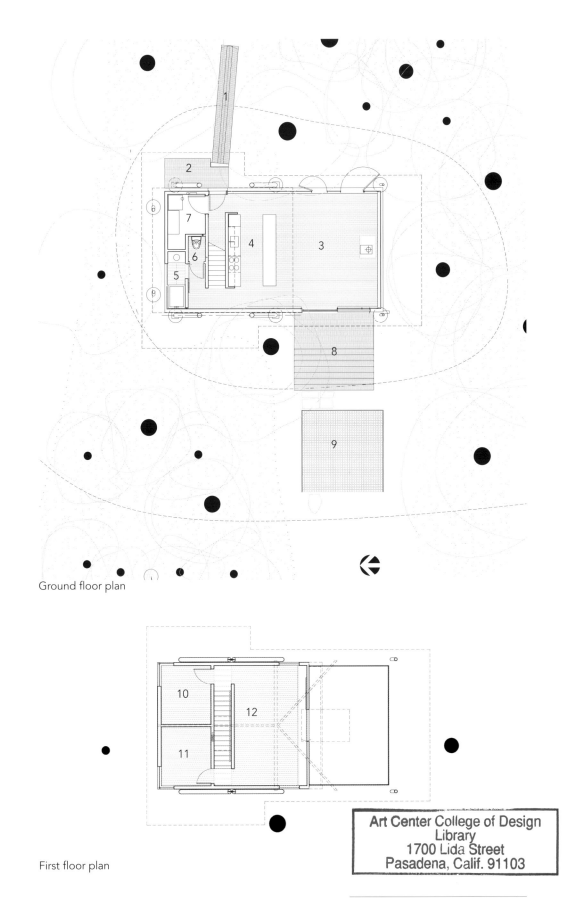

Ground floor plan

First floor plan

The "camp like" living spaces of the platform are protected from the weather by a transparent glass skin that joins the living spaces with the surrounding dense brush. The glazing system, a combination of sealant and vertical steel flat bars that mimic the vertical rhythm of the surrounding trees, wraps around the platform.

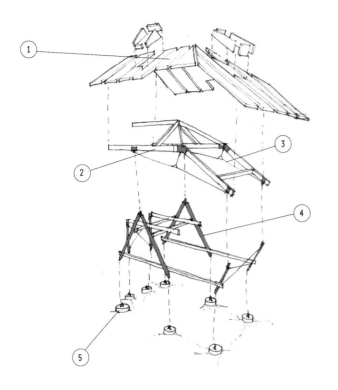

1. Structural insulated panels
2. Glulam beams
3. Steel rods
4. Steel braces
5. Concrete disks

Plan of the main structure

Detail of skylight

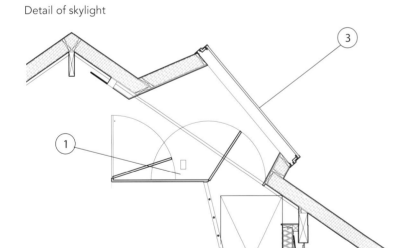

1. Folding sleeping loft
2. Bridge
3. Operable skylight

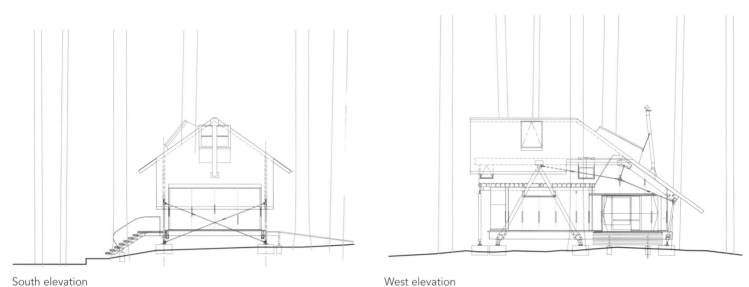

South elevation

West elevation

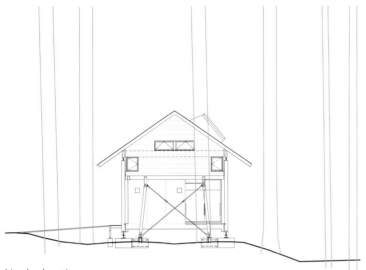

North elevation

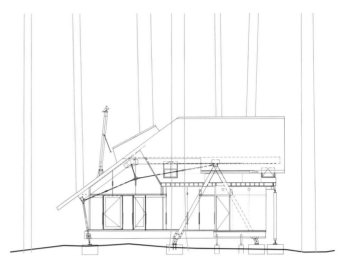

East elevation

Brunsell – Sharples Residence

The Sea Ranch, California

Photographs:
Obie Bowman, Victor Budnik,
Ken Sharples

The terrain where this house is located consists of narrow meadows sandwiched between coastal hills and ocean bluffs, interrupted only by periodic cypress windrows. Cold northerly winds blow through-out the spring and summer. The lot sits on the ocean edge of The Sea Ranch in Sonoma County, California.

The program called for a weekend/retirement house with separate guest and master bedroom wings and a common area for socialization with guests. The heart of the common area is an oversized kitchen island (intended to reduce separation of spaces and people), which always acts as a vital part, if not the focus, of common area activities.

The house responds to the character of the landscape while considering its effect on the community: Besides minimizing loss of the native flora and fauna it strives for visual harmony with the sweep of the coastal hills and responds to the specific conditions to its site: it is an exemplary neighbor and is attuned to the natural forces acting upon it.

The street corner is kept open with soft, low roofed elevations presented to neighbors overlooking the site to view the southerly coastline. The building form, influenced by setback requirements, creates a wind foil which deflects wind up and away from the southerly deck. The meadow displaced by the building footprint has been replaced in the form of an earth covered roof. Only indigenous plants have been used.

The house effectively uses solar space and water heating, natural ventilation, and natural lighting, with a radiant floor backup system. Excess roof water percolates back into the ground, as does much of the water falling on the gravel driveway and parking court. Columns were obtained from a stand of dead Eucalyptus trees. The original fireplace incorporated brick chunks from a grog pile. Predominantly natural materials and natural aging process have been used.

The primary exterior work consists of a spacious set of outdoor spaces including a redwood deck at grade, a concrete terrace sunk below grade, and a hot tub platform. Since these spaces are on the southerly, wind protected side there is almost always an option for outdoor living.

The remodeled interior features a steel plate fireplace front, skylights, built in seating and gallery lighting in the two hallways, and stripped painted trim and doors expose the vertical grain Douglas fir beneath. Much of the façade facing the sea is glazed providing amazing views from the living area and kitchen, as well as affording the house passive heating.

Victor Budnik

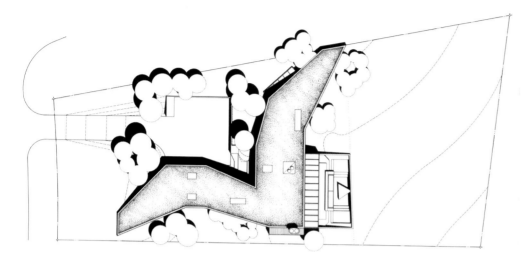

Obie Bowman

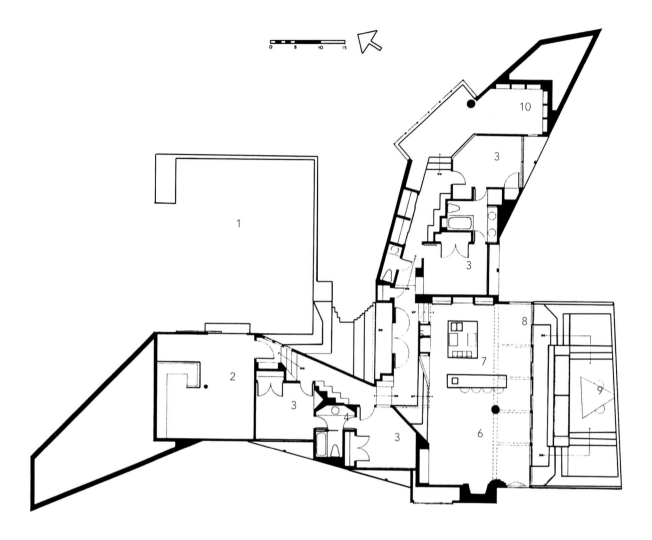

1. Parking yard
2. Shop - garage
3. Bedroom
4. Bath
5. Entry
6. Living
7. Kitchen
8. Dining
9. Deck
10. Study

Victor Budnik

Ken Sharples

Obie Bowman

Obie Bowman

Obie Bowman

Obie Bowman

1. Continuous discharge manifold
2. Solar hot water collector
3. Air intake louvers
4. Brick over slab floor mass

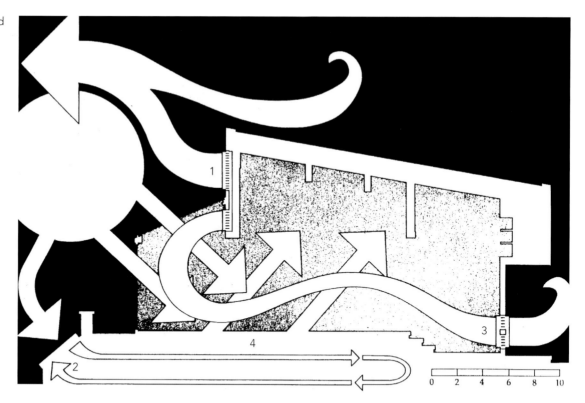

The house effectively uses solar space and water heating, natural ventilation, and natural lighting, with a radiant floor backup system. Excess roof water percolates back into the ground, as does much of the water falling on the gravel driveway and parking court.

Ken Sharples

Obie Bowman

Obie Bowman

Christine's House

Sawyerville, Alabama

Photographs:

Steve Long

Team Designers / builders:

Amy Green |Bullington, Stephen Long

Instructor and Advisor:

Prof. Andrew Freear

Structural Engineer:

Joe Farrugia

This project began with a challenge: to use the red soil, found in abundance in this locality, which is made up of more than 25 % clay. A material known as hybrid adobe was developed to make masonry bricks. This is a combination of newspaper, water, earth and Portland cement and, thanks to the addition of newspaper, has the advantage of being lighter than adobe, provides better insulation and is highly cost effective.

The project's driving force became two hybrid adobe walls. A sequence of progression is defined that goes through several stages, from public to increasingly private: the large shared green space becomes a more private yard the other side of the eastern adobe wall. This eastern wall rises gently with the ground, mirroring a ramp that slopes up with the landscape to the screened front porch. This block wall then stretches across the front porch and into the living space, mediating between exterior and interior.

The eastern earth wall rises above the interior floor, with glass bridging the gap between the top of the wall and the roof. This glazing lets natural light into the interior, while allowing glimpses of the surrounding landscape from the interior. Another thick adobe wall cuts through the center of the house, stopping short of the ceiling. Light from a clerestory illuminates the wall's texture, while air circulates over it and through a break in its surface. This central wall is present in each of the four main rooms – the living and kitchen areas and each main bedroom – and has been left without a veneer. Both the eastern and central block wall are also freed from being load-bearing; a series of concrete columns enveloped by the adobe blocks bears the weight of the roof's steel beams.

The family is connected through a series of defined spaces. Public and private areas in the house's interior are separated by the central block wall, while transparency from front to back unites the spaces on each side of this wall. The eastern adobe wall creates horizontal space while the wind tower rises to enclose space vertically. The kitchen is directly centered over the tower, which is used for natural air ventilation throughout the house, and allows an abundance of natural light into the space. This area becomes the central point of family gathering and activity, a space cradled between the two earth walls. The material palette for the house was purposefully limited to preserve simplicity and clarity in the design. The earth was viewed as the most important material, while glass was used for transparency and lightness. Cedar and metal were secondary materials, with cedar being primarily an interior finish and corrugated metal being used as roofing as well as the exterior finish for the tower.

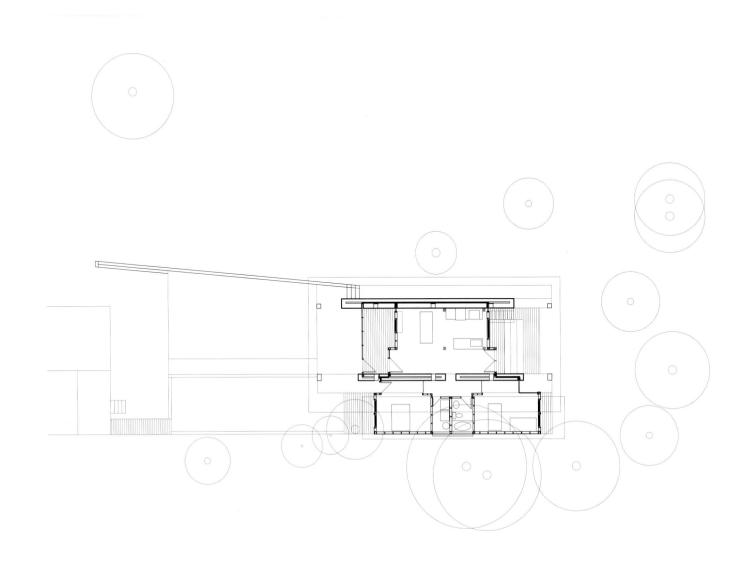

The house was oriented so that a dense tree line provides shade during most of the day. It was opened to the north and south to let in light and activity, while the east and west sides became solid to preserve privacy and protect the inhabitants from the most intense sun.

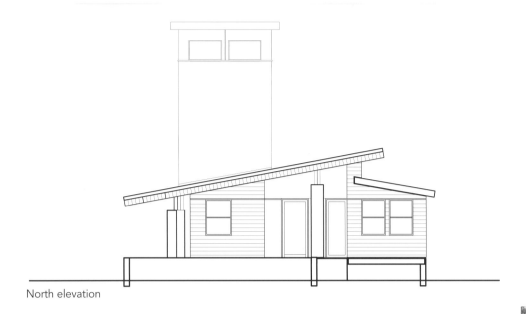

North elevation

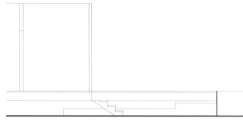

West elevation

South elevation

The material palette for the house was purposefully limited to preserve simplicity and clarity in the design. The earth was viewed as the most important material, while glass was used for transparency and lightness. Cedar and metal were secondary materials, with cedar being primarily an interior finish and corrugated metal being used as roofing as well as the exterior finish for the tower.

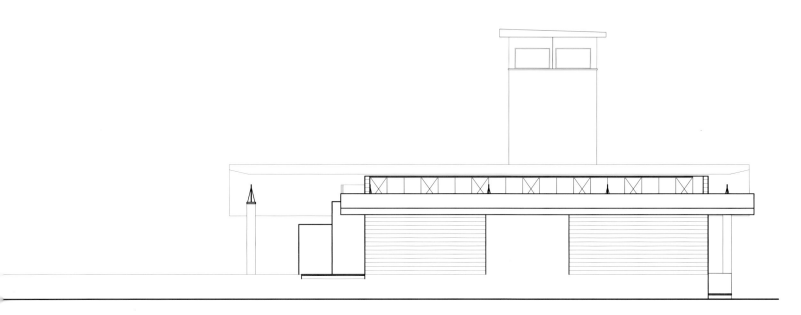

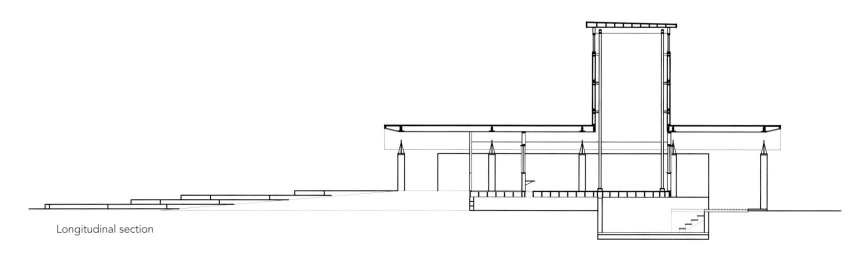

Longitudinal section

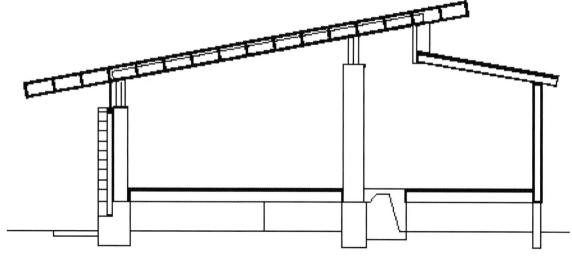

Cross section

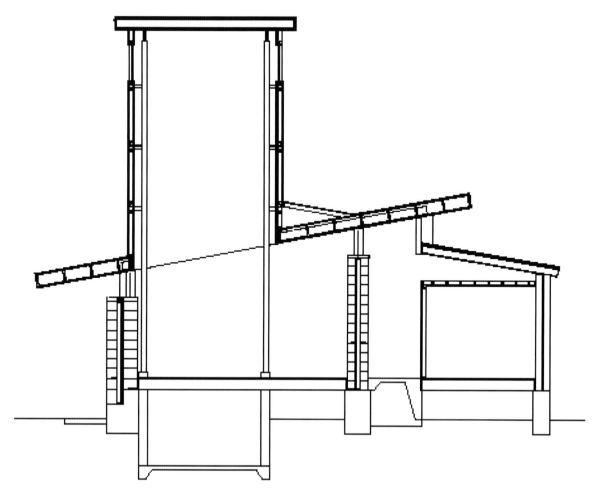

Cross section at the tower

Desert Nomad House

Tucson, Arizona

Photographs:
Undine Pröhl

Rick Joy, was the recipient of the 2004 Smithsonian Cooper-Hewitt National Design Award. He has specialized in re-evaluating and redefining the traditional building techniques of the American Southwest. Acknowledging the influence of such artists as Richard Serra and James Turrell, Rick Joy's orchestration of light, color and geometry, by the sensitive use of rammed earth, glass and steel, is aimed to underline the visual environment of the Arizona desert.

Nestled in a secluded bowl-like formation in the land, striving for low impact and equilibrium among the saguaros, the three boxes have landed in their rightful place. Opportunities for dramatic views surround the site, so a particular angle was carefully selected for each primary space, after studying the possible orientations.

The house is divided into three zones. In the main living space there is an intense early evening view to the southeast, where the setting sun highlights a large rocky hill; the low-lying landscape in the foreground lies in the shadow of the mountains behind. As night falls, the city lights of Tucson emerge. For the bedroom, the rising sun illuminates a particularly stunning rock face at the top of the mountains to the southwest. The reflected light backlights the saguaros and ocotillo in the foreground. An outcrop of rock overgrown with saguaros makes a still life to be enjoyed from glazed side of the small den.

To enhance the experience of each space and view, the three different zones have been given an individual box-like structure with a single opening through which to experience the corresponding sunlight event. Each box is raised above the ground and solid concrete blocks step down to the level of the footpaths that cross the space between the cubicles, reinforcing their feeling of isolation. The fragility of the site also prompted this idea, which permits water and animals to flow freely underneath. The forms have an elusive appearance in the landscape. Like a group of hunter's blinds, their presence remains nearly unnoticed from the surrounding area.

Architects:
Rick Joy Architects
Principal:
Rick Joy
Project architect:
Andy Tinucci (phase 1),
Cade Hayes (phase 2)
Design team:
Rick Joy, Andy Tinucci,
Chelsea Grassinger, Cade Hayes
Engineer:
SW Structural
General contractor:
Rick Joy Architects
Cabinetry:
Seva Vasilyev
Carpentry:
WJ Lang, Chris Helgeson,
Everett Melton, Franz Buhler
Plumber:
Richard Mayers
Electricians:
United Electric
Steel:
Parsons Steel

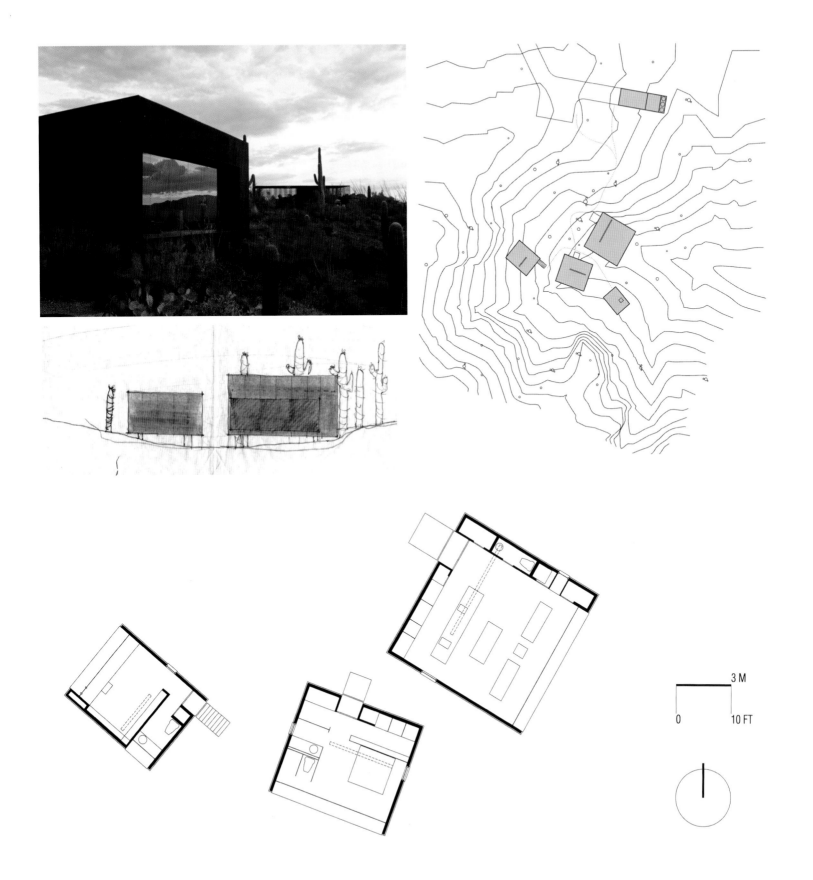

3 M

0 — 10 FT

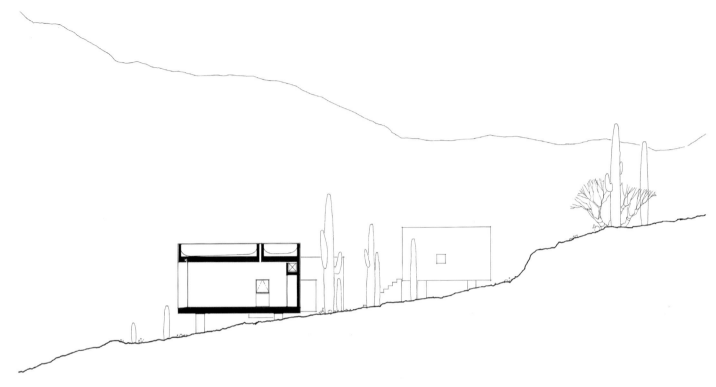

Jones Studio, Inc

Jones-Johnson Residencia

Phoenix, Arizona

Photographs:
Timothy Hursley, Sally Schoolmaster

No one wanted the 1 acre mountain preserve land with a natural 16 000 acre backyard because, everyone knew that the proximity of the huge, neighbourhood chlorinating tank was unacceptable.

Just a few simple moves created a rammed earth form that integrated the beautiful mountain views due north, with a softly daylit family gathering space. And each cylindrically composed outdoor room made friends with the Mother cylinder. The house fits between the existing water tank, the mountain preserve and the pink stucco, red tile roof neighbouring homes. It's cylindrical site walls and north-south facing fenestration strategically capture mountain views while masking unwanted sights of the water tank and adjacent neighbourhood. The rotated concrete, bubble block walls used in the front and back of the house afford privacy without sacrificing air circulation.

Known by the community as "The Dirt House", the residence reintroduces rammed earth, a 1000 year old building technology, in a contemporary, resource-efficient way. To create the rammed earth wall, scoops of barely-moistened dirt from the site, mixed with 3 % Portland cement, are loaded into plywood forms in lifts of eight inches. A hand-held pneumatic tamper compacts the dirt into a rock-hard six-inch layer. This process is repeated until the desired wall height is achieved. The forms are removed, resulting in a very solid, energy-efficient wall system. The rammed walls of this residence are 2 feet thick and 18 feet tall. The heat will conduct through compacted dirt at a rate of 1 inch per hour, so, the interior surface maintains a constant room temperature throughout the year. Most of the construction materials used in this home have significant recycled content and/or are resource-efficient materials. A few notable examples are: plywood glued together with toxin-free adhesives, low to no VOC paints (actually, there is almost no paint on the project) high performance glazing, engineered composite framing lumber, rusted steel wall cladding, and concrete block manufactured with fly ash.

Extensive overhangs, a rusted steel louver, and careful solar orientation ensure complete natural day lighting with responsible sun control.

Landscaping in the yard is naturally irrigated by a rainwater-harvesting system. Rain water is directed gently from the roof to the desert floor by a stainless steel chain-link hung from rusted, black iron steel plates. The roof is pitched toward the large scupper projecting from the stair tower. Rainwater clings to "rain-chains" and is deflected into an 18-foot diameter holding area by large concrete sphere splash blocks. When the detention area fills, the water overflows into the landscaping.

Every habitable space is bathed in natural, filtered daylight, substantially decreasing the need for electric lighting during the daytime hours.

230 Jones Studio, Inc

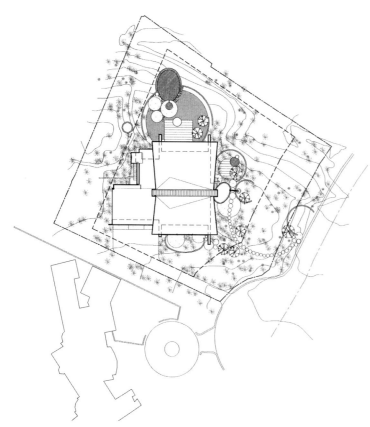

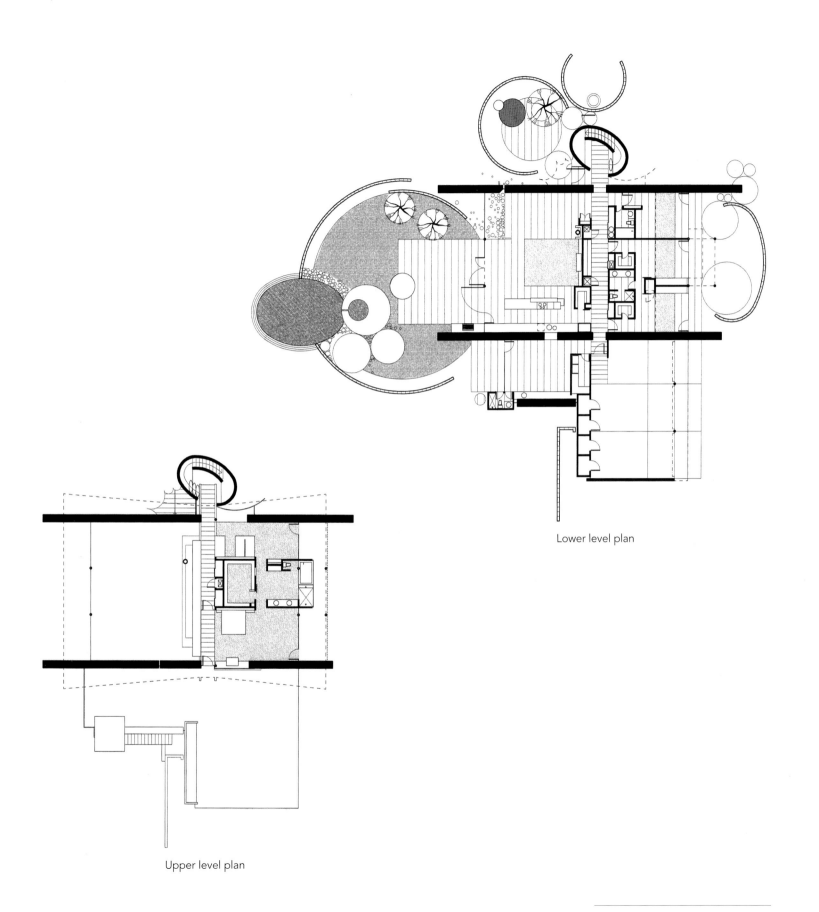

Lower level plan

Upper level plan

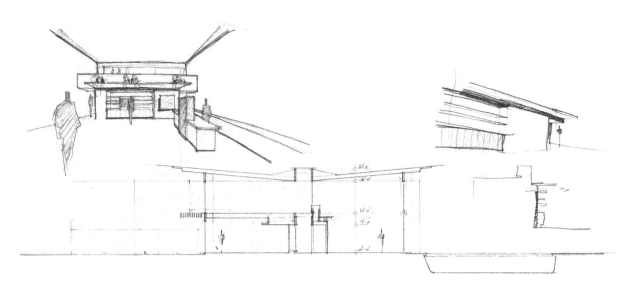

234   Jones Studio, Inc

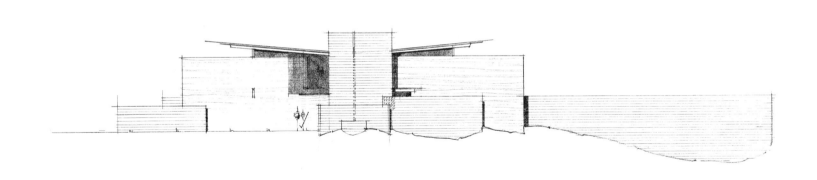

The main space of the dwelling combines all the public zones of the dwelling, including the kitchen and the dining room. The transversal bracing system, right, crosses the large glazed window providing stability, support for the lighting, and allowing good views of the mountains.